# Journey Through the Furnace

# Journey Through the Furnace
## God is There!

Understand the effects of child sexual abuse on primary survivors and the impact on secondary survivors - their families and those who love them

**Sharron Dansby**

Journey Through the Furnace…God is There!
Copyright ©2017 by Sharron Dansby
Visit www.sharrondansby.com and www.maxgodswoman.org

All scripture quotations, unless otherwise indicated, are taken from the *New King James* Version, Copyright 1982 by Thomas Nelson, Inc.
Used by permission. All rights reserved
Scripture quotations noted (KJV) are taken from the
*King James* Version of the Bible.
ISBN-13: 9781979506151
ISBN-10: 1979506159

No part of this publication may be reproduced, stored in a retrieval system, or transmitted in any form by any means – electronic, mechanical, photocopy, recording, or otherwise – without the prior permission of the publisher, except as provided by U.S.A. copyright law.

Edited by Paula Wynn, Verbal Radiance Editorial Services

*In memory of
my beloved sister, Precious,
who longed for but was unable to see
the completion of this book*

*Sharron Dansby has truly captured the essence of God's mercy in transforming broken lives through the power of Jesus Christ. Her story of pain, betrayal, and confusion transcends gender, culture, and generation. It portraits the danger of keeping secrets best exposed and shows how God's amazing grace turns trials into triumphs.*
*- PB Wynn*

# Contents

Acknowledgments · · · · · · · · · · · · · · · · · · · · · · · · · · · xi
Introduction · · · · · · · · · · · · · · · · · · · · · · · · · · · · · · · · xiii

Part I: The Furnace · · · · · · · · · · · · · · · · · · · · · · · · · · · · · · · · 1
  Chapter 1    Her Cry for Help · · · · · · · · · · · · · · · 3
  Chapter 2    Breaking the Silence · · · · · · · · · · · · · 9
  Chapter 3    What's Wrong With Me? · · · · · · · · · · · · 15
  Chapter 4    Mothers Cry Too · · · · · · · · · · · · · · · · 27
Part II: Heat in the Furnace · · · · · · · · · · · · · · · · · · · · · · · · 37
  Chapter 5    Lonely, But Not Alone · · · · · · · · · · · · 39
  Chapter 6    A Family Affair · · · · · · · · · · · · · · · · · 47
  Chapter 7    Whose Fault Is It? · · · · · · · · · · · · · · · 61
Part III: Malleable for Shaping · · · · · · · · · · · · · · · · · · · · · 69
  Chapter 8    Me, Love Him? · · · · · · · · · · · · · · · · · 71
  Chapter 9    You're Forgiven · · · · · · · · · · · · · · · · · 80
  Chapter 10   Take Me Back! · · · · · · · · · · · · · · · · · 85
Part IV: Magnificent Product · · · · · · · · · · · · · · · · · · · · · · 95
  Chapter 11   Oh No, Not Again! · · · · · · · · · · · · · · · 97
  Chapter 12   Pain, Pain, Go Away! · · · · · · · · · · · · · 110
  Chapter 13   For A Purpose · · · · · · · · · · · · · · · · · · 119
  Chapter 14   Now That I Know · · · · · · · · · · · · · · · 126

Conclusion of the Matter · · · · · · · · · · · · · · · · · · · · · · 139
End Notes · · · · · · · · · · · · · · · · · · · · · · · · · · · · · · · · · · 141

# Acknowledgments

I give praise and thanks to my Glorious Heavenly Father for choosing me to travel through this journey of affliction and for bringing countless precious friends into my life to love me and help me through my journey.

I'm thankful for my testimony and the opportunity to help others who have gone through and prevent some to never experience child sexual abuse.

With deepest appreciation to:
My children and sisters who suffered along with me and assisted in writing this book, sharing their most intimate secrets to help others;

Pastors James Earls, Allen McFarland, Leroy Ricks Sr., and Edwin Goodwin, longtime pastors and friends, for their sound biblical teaching and examples of "stepping out on faith and trusting God regardless of whatever happens in life;"

Pastor John K. Jenkins Sr., and First Lady Trina Jenkins, First Baptist Church of Glenarden, for their teachings that inspired me to embrace <u>my story</u> " <u>it's not for me but for someone else who needs to hear it</u>"

Rebecca Osaigbovo, Deborah Leaner, and Dr. Celeste Owens, PhD, friends and great authors, who inspired me to write my story;

And last but not least, Charles Dansby, who took my hand in marriage in our mature years, and demonstrated God's love to me and my family.

# Introduction

In the beginning of our lives someone records our birth and at the end someone records our death. Between those two periods of time is a dash that represents the life we lived here on this earth. Each of us has a story to tell about some significant event in our lives. This book is my story. It's my journey through child sexual abuse and how that trauma affected my life, my marriage, and most of all, my family relationships.

Imagine an eight year old girl playing alone and an adult male befriends her only to misuse his authority and sexually abuse her. She is left feeling violated, scared, and emotionally tormented. Even though the girl needs it very much, she receives no therapy and lives life feeling she is "damaged goods." There's no emotional support for her because the abuse was kept secret. No crime is reported so the perpetrator goes unpunished. What a tragedy! But this is typical of child sexual abuse and it's my story.

This book is about my journey through affliction, which I refer to as "the furnace". It reveals intimate aspects of my personal life and how sexual abuse impacted our family. As a victim of child sexual abuse, the consequent lack of self-worth, and ensuing low self-esteem affected the decisions I made. Desperation for love and acceptance resulted in marrying a man I thought would be the answer to my happiness. Instead, the dynamics of the love we once shared turned to the ultimate betrayal - our daughter being molested by her own father.

Although I was a Christian at the time, trying to console my young daughter after the sexual abuse while dealing with the emotional struggles

# Introduction

of my other children who were traumatized by the incest, and confronting suppressed feelings from my own child sexual abuse was heart wrenching. My story is a journey filled with struggles, challenges, lessons, and victories. It progresses from shame and betrayal to trust, respect, self-worth, love, and forgiveness.

This journey covers a span of thirty years. The hurts, pains, and betrayal I experienced led me to a closer relationship with the Lord. It was through the "furnace" experience that I was transformed from having a "victim mentality" to being made "healthy and whole." Through this journey I learned how to overcome and live a joyful and victorious life. Although I sometimes struggled with my faith in God, I was determined to be obedient to Him, and He blessed me with a challenging and rewarding life. Through Him I received healing, both emotionally and spiritually.

I have opened the windows of my heart so that others may know that no matter how dark the night, God is always there - even when we don't feel His presence. He has a plan for our lives and often takes us on a journey through the furnace to draw us closer to Him.

# Part I
# The Furnace

*When I think about dark places and tough situations, I am reminded of the blacksmith and his furnace. I am intrigued by how the blacksmith takes a piece of iron, encloses it into the structure of the furnace, and applies extreme heat until the iron is pliable - able to be molded and shaped into a quality product that the blacksmith desires.*

*I often thought of myself as iron, strong and unyielding. I thought I was strong because I had endured the trauma of sexual abuse, but actually I was 'hard.' I had built an emotional wall around me hoping to avoid pain by keeping others at a distance. But God, the Master Blacksmith who created me in His image, knew everything about me and what I needed.*

*He led me through a furnace experience that I might reflect the beauty of His handiwork and reach my designed destiny. During the journey I had to 'remove my mask' and deal with my pain. I learned that suffering is a part of life and although I couldn't escape being hurt, God was with me in all of it.*

CHAPTER 1

# Her Cry for Help

As we journey through life there are many things that grab our attention, but none is more piercing than a child's cry for help. Images of children dying of starvation, children physically abused or neglected, children crying because they feel unloved and rejected by others, children being emotionally abused, or children's tears over great disappointments or unfulfilled promises, stir our hearts and challenge us to do something to relieve them of their pain and suffering. It's always alarming when children are abused because it shouldn't hurt to be a child.

It's fairly easy to identify child abuse when we see broken bones, bruises, or malnutrition. Even though it's less detectable than physical abuse, sexual abuse can be just as or even more devastating. Some children suffer in silence, afraid to disclose the abuse to anyone. Others make it known, only to experience rejection and shame. But thank God for the adults who hear the children's cry and proceed to do something about it.

Children are crying out for help and our involvement could change a life forever. Making a difference starts with one child at a time and that child could be your very own. That was my situation!

## Her Letter – My Pivotal Moment
My three children and I had just returned home from Sunday evening church service and proceeded to our bedrooms to prepare for bed. As I stood beside my dresser, there was a knock on my door. Allison, my eleven year old daughter, entered my room and handed me a handwritten letter.

# Her Cry for Help

Without a word she turned and left the room. I had no idea what was going on but cautiously opened the folded paper. With sickening bewilderment, I read the details of the letter revealing that she was being sexually abused.

Allison used words which were explicit and anatomically correct, even though she drew a line through some of them. I read the letter several times, my heart pounding dangerously within me. I had no doubt she was telling the truth even though I had difficulty believing this was really happening. I understood this was Allison's desperate cry for help.

Dumbfounded, I just stood there holding the letter in my hand. I wanted to interrogate Allison to get the rest of the facts like: how did this happen, what caused it and most of all – where was I when all this happened? But all I could do was stand there, reading the letter again and again. I was mortified because she also disclosed that my husband, her biological father, was the perpetrator! I took a deep breath and cried out "My God, I need help RIGHT now! This is my family!"

I called Allison back into my room to discuss her letter. I saw the sad expression on her face, the one I'd seen so many times before but hadn't known why. I had reasoned that she was just going through pre-adolescence. Allison began to talk and reiterate the facts, but with very little emotion.

"How long has this been going on?" I asked.

"For some time," she responded.

"Why didn't you tell me before now?" I asked weakly.

"I tried but I didn't want to hurt you," she replied.

I didn't know exactly what Allison called "for some time" but I didn't want to put her through any further interrogation at that time. Neither, did I fully understand why she felt compelled to protect me when she was the one in danger. I should have been protecting her. I loved Allison and she knew that I did. I always believed we had a good mother-daughter relationship and that we could talk about anything, which made this situation even more painful. As Allison stood looking at the floor, she asked a profound question "Momma, why did God let this happen to me?" I couldn't answer because I had the same concern.

Standing in my bedroom with Allison's letter in my hand, I heard Allison's cry for help and I knew I had to do something. I certainly couldn't ignore the problem. Richard, my husband, was due to return home from his weekend drill with the National Guard so I moved quickly. It was critical for me to talk to someone before confronting Richard. Talking to Richard about sensitive issues hadn't been successful in the past, and this issue was much worse than anything we'd previously experienced. I couldn't handle this alone. I needed help.

The first person that came to my mind was my pastor whom I turned to for counseling so many times before. Not wanting to break down emotionally in front of my children, I folded the letter and tucked it into my jacket. I did not want Allison to hear me reading her letter to someone else, so I left the house and used the public pay phone in front of the 7-Eleven convenience store near my home.

My conversation with Pastor Roger evolved into more than the usual counseling, prayer, and encouragement he had given me numerous times before. This night was different. My family was out of control and I had reached a point of desperation. With my heart pounding outrageously, I read Allison's letter to Pastor Roger. His words pierced me as he informed me that I must report the incident to the proper authorities. I had no previous experience with reporting child abuse and didn't know where to start so Pastor Roger recommended I get legal advice and kindly provided the name of an attorney. I held the phone for a few speechless seconds then assured him I wanted to protect Allison and would make the call the first thing in the morning. At the conclusion of the conversation and after a word of prayer asking for God's guidance, power, and protection through this ordeal, I hung up and hurriedly headed home.

As I drove toward the house I couldn't help but wonder how I was going to approach Richard. I didn't think my heart could take any more pain. Our twelve years of marriage could best be characterized as full of deceit, dishonesty, distrust, and infidelity. From the outside we looked like any normal family, but we were struggling to survive. Richard and I lived in the same house but were emotionally estranged from one another; we

# Her Cry for Help

went through the motions of marriage but hurt and anger caused us to barely tolerate one another. Even though I'd experienced so many disappointments and unfulfilled expectations in the marriage, I had little reason to suspect Richard was capable of incest.

Before I parked the car in the driveway, God gave me wisdom. I was not to confront Richard that night but to wait until after I talked to the attorney. Thankful that Richard wasn't home yet, I checked on the children and found the boys playing in their room instead of getting ready for bed. Allison was in her bed with the covers pulled tightly around her neck. After getting the boys settled, I went into the living room and sat on the sofa. I just wanted to think. I had no desire to call anyone, not even my own family members or the friends at church who shared so much of our lives together. I just needed to meditate on all that was happening. It was all so unbelievable…it was a nightmare, except I was wide awake. The perpetrator in this situation wasn't just any man…it was my husband who violated our child.

Sitting there in the dimly lit room, wrapped in my deepest thoughts, I reflected over God's promises and held on to the fact that the Lord is God. Knowing that He is all powerful, I cried out "Lord I need you so much. Please help me now!" Just as I concluded my prayer Richard walked into the house. Immediately he sensed something was wrong with me. He asked if I was okay, but I couldn't answer him. Sitting there and staring into space, I remained silent.

Richard started toward the kitchen but turned around and came back into the living room. He did something very strange. Never one to be overly affectionate, he sat down on the floor next to my legs and laid his head on my lap. This wasn't something he'd done before which made me think that he knew that I knew what he was doing to Allison.

I remained motionless. Neither of us said anything. We sat in that position for what seemed like an hour. I felt so empty inside…no emotion at all. Then, without saying a word, Richard got up and went to bed while I remained on the sofa. Later I walked down the hall and peeked into our bedroom. I stared at Richard who was soundly asleep. I wondered how he could do such an awful thing and go about his daily routine day after day as if nothing had happened. This news was so unbelievable. I was scared and felt so alone.

I went back to my spot on the sofa to commune with the Source of all my strength. I talked to the Lord and cried "Oh Dear GOD –this is my family - what a mess! The enemy is trying to destroy us. Give me the strength to do what needs to be done. My little girl didn't deserve this."

It was so tempting to be angry with God and lash out against Him for this injustice, but I fought those feelings because I needed Him too much at that moment to turn away from Him. Who else could I turn to? It was God's power working in my life that brought me this far and I had to believe He would work in this situation also – I just didn't want to go through it.

I wished the pain in my heart would magically disappear or better yet, I would wake up and discover it was only a bad dream, a horrible nightmare. All I could do was sit there and repeat over again, "Oh God, help me. This burden is too heavy for me. How can I help Allison if I can't get myself together?"

## *Whispers on My Journey*

### *On my journey through the furnace*
### *I heard a whisper –*
### *"Be vigilant."*

*I prided myself on being a good parent. Being watchful and avoiding danger is what I had been doing. I kept close watch over my children. I taught them not to talk to strangers or go anywhere with people they didn't know. I set up safety measures to keep them safe around the house so they wouldn't hurt themselves. I seldom allowed them to spend the night over someone else's house even when I knew the people. I took them to church and gave them a Christian education. I tried to do what was best for them.*

*So when Allison asked "Why did God let this happen to me?" I understood why she questioned God. I, too, wondered why God allowed this to happen to her. I had a hard time understanding it myself, let alone being able to explain it to my child. I reflected back to when Allison was four years old and asked "Momma, does it hurt when Jesus comes in your heart?" Allison was such an obedient child, enthusiastic and interested in God's word. As I explained God's plan of salvation to my young daughter, she prayed and asked Jesus into her life. I taught her that God is love. That He is always present and has all power. That God is good and kind. That He protects and watches over us….yet she was sexually abused.*

*Was I oblivious to any sexual misconduct or inappropriate behavior because my children were young? I taught my children a lot of things, but I hadn't discussed the subject of sex with them nor had I taken measures to keep them from being alone with their father. Why would I? He was their daddy. I never witnessed him behaving in an inappropriate or sexual way with the children. On the contrary, Richard was usually stern and many times was emotionally detached from them.*

*What signs had I missed? Someone said "ignorance is bliss" but it's not. What I didn't know about incest ended up hurting us all, especially Allison.*

CHAPTER 2

# Breaking the Silence

The night Allison handed me the letter pertaining to the sexual abuse was very long. Sitting on that sofa I anxiously thought about the challenges I had to face the next day. I wanted morning to come quickly. I wanted to get the legalities over. After Richard left for work I half-heartedly got the kids ready for school. I braced myself to contact the lawyer that Pastor Roger had referred.

As soon as the office opened, I called the attorney to schedule an appointment. After learning the nature of my call, I was instructed to come into his office immediately and to bring Allison's letter with me. I didn't call anyone to accompany me, not Pastor Roger, not my family, and not my friends at church. Once the children were off to school, I quickly rushed to the attorney's office with Allison's letter tucked in my purse.

From the moment I received the letter from Allison until the time I reached the attorney's office I had controlled my emotions pretty well. Sitting in the attorney's office discussing such an intimate and shameful matter with a total stranger released the explosion that had been building inside me. I began to tremble and shake uncontrollably. My fingers were actually jumping up and down on the chair as I unsuccessfully tried to hold it and appear calm. I could not stop the flow of tears. When the attorney finished reading the letter, he came over and put his hand on mine.

"We have enough evidence to proceed." He continued, "We need to take your daughter to Child Protective Service (CPS) to officially report this abuse." I felt so ashamed, and silently prayed, "Dear God how can I do this alone?" I knew I was doing the right thing and God was with me, but I was still scared. The lawyer volunteered to go with me to get Allison from school and to accompany us to CPS. I didn't know if he was just being considerate or wanted to ensure that I reported the abuse. It didn't matter. I was so grateful for his presence.

We arrived at Allison's school and signed her out for the remainder of the day. Outside the school the attorney asked Allison a few more questions concerning the letter. In his mild manner, he reassured Allison this process would put an end to the sexual abuse. I could see Allison was nervous so I held her hand to calm her. Fear was all over Allison's face by the time we arrived at CPS. A stern-faced social worker greeted us and glanced over Allison's letter. "Who lined through the words describing the sexual body parts?" she wanted to know. I responded that it was Allison.

In spite of the fact she had Allison's letter in hand she informed me that she still needed to interview Allison and hear the story directly from her. Motioning Allison to follow her to a back office, she instructed me to wait in another room so she could talk to Allison alone. Allison was scared and I didn't like the idea that I couldn't be with her. Neither of us was prepared for this. I wondered what type of questions she would ask Allison. I felt helpless as I watched my little girl go into a room alone with a stranger to discuss something so personal. It only took a short time for the interview then the CPS worker told me she had enough evidence for Richard's arrest.

Anger, fear, resentment, shame, betrayal…I'm not sure what else I felt. I fought back tears as I thought about Richard being arrested. He had never been in any trouble with the law before so I had no reason to believe he would resist arrest. However, it unnerved me as I visualized police cars with flashing lights in front of the house while officers handcuffed Richard in the presence of my children and all the neighbors.

Not wanting my children to experience any more embarrassment than absolutely necessary, I pleaded with the CPS counselor not to arrest Richard at our house. She assured me that once Richard received her call he would be given the opportunity to turn himself in. However, she warned "If he doesn't come into the office of his own free will, we will execute a warrant for his arrest and apprehend him." I prayed, I mean I really prayed with all my heart, that Richard would turn himself in.

Upon leaving the building and approaching the car, I noticed Allison had been crying and that she was emotionally drained. I couldn't help but blame myself for not protecting her. I was her mother and I was supposed to protect my daughter. Trying to relieve her pain, I hugged her and reassured her that we were doing the right thing. Still, I had no idea what to anticipate next. I knew however, it was going to be a very difficult process to go through. Nevertheless, I wanted to press on for this was the only way to stop the sexual abuse. She had suffered so much and I was going to put an end to it. I smiled at Allison and told her that I was so proud of her for disclosing the incest. As I looked at her I thought "What a brave young lady!"

The more I thought about what Richard did to Allison, the worse I felt. I was angry about what already happened and fearful about the road ahead. Most of the day had been spent between the attorney's office and CPS. Allison and I went home and for the next couple hours I watched the clock. It was approaching the end of Richard's workday. I wasn't sure if he would turn himself in or try to come home. While fearfully waiting and in anticipation of the CPS phone call, my mind jumped from one thought to another.

I didn't know of anyone who had reported sexual abuse before. I was "charting new waters" and was certainly a pioneer for our family. I thought about Allison and how scared she was when she talked to the CPS worker. I wondered if Social Services would take my children away from me. I wondered how I was going to tell the boys about this incident and that their father was probably going to jail. I had no idea how my family would respond or how his family would react. My thoughts were interrupted when the phone rang. I sighed with relief when the voice on the other end said, "We got him!" Richard had turned himself in.

Nothing I encountered in reporting the abuse was easy or pleasant. It wasn't easy to watch my daughter withdraw from me and seclude herself in her room and own world. It wasn't easy watching my two other children react and display defiant behavior because of the unrest at home. It wasn't easy for me to live a life where everyone knew my family's deepest shame. I didn't want people to know my daughter was violated or what happened in our home but the word was out whether I liked it or not. Although I had reported the sexual abuse, I still felt uncomfortable discussing it with anyone. I didn't want Allison to be further humiliated. Neither did I want to be blamed for the abuse or accused of not being a good mother.

I'm thankful my faith in God kept me from going into a deep depression. I held on to the fact that revealing the secret meant the enemy wouldn't have power over us through this situation. We wouldn't have to live a lie or be fearful that sometime in the future someone else would reveal our family secret. But most of all, Allison would be able to receive help from those trained to deal with these type of situations. I knew that reporting the abuse was the right thing to do.

## Legal Support

In April 1982 when we reported the sexual abuse to CPS, the government was doing more to make the public aware of child sexual abuse and to punish perpetrators. According to Wikipedia in the 1970s child sexual abuse became a public issue. Legal actions became more prevalent with the enactment of Child Abuse Prevention and Treatment Act (CAPTA) in 1974 in conjunction with the creation of the National Center for Child Abuse and Neglect. In 1979, the National Abuse Coalition was created to pressure Congress into establishing more sexual abuse laws.

By 2008, the U. S. Department of Health and Human Services, Administration for Children & Families, reported 758,289 cases of child maltreatment (abuse and neglect) that fiscal year. As alarming as these numbers are, they don't take into consideration the number of unreported cases and repeated abuses year after year. The Child Maltreatment 2008 report indicated 9.1 percent of the maltreatments were classified as sexual abuse and some sexually abused victims likely sustained other types of abuses as well. CAPTA defined sexual abuse as inappropriate sexual behaviors that ranged from sexual contact (oral, anal, or genital penetration or genital contact without penetration, fondling of breast and buttocks) to non-touching (indecent exposure, exposing a child to pornography, internet crimes, or other sexually exploitative activities).[1]

The majority of perpetrators were known by their victims, either related or responsible for the care of the child. A large percentage of sexual abuse involved incest among family members. Research indicated that sexual abuse involved various degrees of violence and emotional trauma and didn't have to be violent to be dangerous.[2] Many perpetrators befriended their victims and/or used the power of their position as their weapon. This is what happened in Allison's case. Richard didn't hold a gun to her head or knife to her throat, but he abused his parental authority to rob her of her innocence.

Richard was reported to CPS and the family courts were involved because he committed the crime against a family member. I was made aware of the civil penalties that could include loss of custody or parental rights, even for me as a spouse if I didn't cooperate with the authorities. The criminal penalties for Richard could involve imprisonment, fines, requirement to register as a sex offender, and probation or parole restrictions.

## *Whispers on My Journey*

**On my journey through the furnace
I heard a whisper –
"Governing authorities that exist are appointed by God."
Romans 13:1**

*When it became unbearable for Allison to keep the secret any longer, she gave me the letter disclosing the incest expecting that I would do something to help her. Although I didn't know what to do, I wasn't going to cover up the incest or ignore it. My daughter would not grow up feeling that I didn't believe her or that I didn't love her enough to take action. Calling the attorney was the best thing I could have done because he made me aware of the laws regarding sexual abuse. I was too close to the problem and was very thankful there were laws to govern the process and send a message to Richard that his actions would not be tolerated by society or go unpunished.*

*I made the right decision to report the abuse but nothing could erase the pain in my heart from the guilt that I somehow permitted the incest to happen because it occurred in my house. I had to move past my feelings. Not knowing what to expect from one day to the next kept me depending on God and asking for courage to allow the messy legal process to work for us. I didn't have a choice in how matters were handled and there were repercussions and penalties if I failed to cooperate. I didn't agree with certain aspects of the process but submitted to the authorities because the laws were there to protect my family.*

CHAPTER 3

# What's Wrong With Me?

After Allison's sexual abuse, I reflected over my life and the path that led to this place. I remembered my childhood and asking the questions "What's wrong with me? Why me? What's so terrible about me that bad things continue to happen to me?" I often wondered if I had done something wrong and if God was punishing me. In the deep recesses of my heart I knew that was false reasoning, but the pain and lack of understanding the situation made me ask those negative questions again and again.

Allison's letter started a chain reaction of events in my life. One of the benefits of reporting the incest was being ordered to attend family and individual counseling. I'm not sure I would have chosen counseling on my own accord but it was an opportunity to talk about my painful childhood, including the feelings I masked and previously denied.

During my counseling sessions I was asked several times if I had been molested as a child. My answer was always a quick "no." I had pushed the trauma so far away from my memory that I truly denied it happened. But after a few sessions, one night while lying in bed I began to have flashbacks of my child sexual abuse - the secret I had kept for many years. I remembered feeling violated, afraid, guilty, and ashamed. I was glad to have a "safe" place where I could discuss my feelings because the memories were painful and I couldn't do it alone.

## Childhood Pain
Unlike Allison, as a child I didn't have the courage to report the sexual abuse that happened to me. I was too scared. It was through counseling

## What's Wrong With Me?

that I was finally able to face my own feelings and identify with Allison's feelings about her painful experience. Being afraid to report my child sexual abuse wasn't without merit. My early childhood years were characterized by fear and insecurities.

My earliest recollection of pain was at five years of age. Mom and Dad were separated and my three sisters and I lived with my father in Franklin, Pennsylvania. Dad was a preacher with a small congregation and a dishonorable reputation of being a "lady's man." His girlfriend and a few women in the church did all they could to help their young, twenty eight year old pastor raise his four young children. Daddy had problems but we knew that he loved us and those ladies in the church loved us too.

One of my fondest memories was being alone and playing with Lady, my collie dog, beside the brook behind our house. One day, quite unexpectedly, Mom showed up with social workers to take all four of us girls away from Daddy. Though the second oldest, just nineteen months younger than my sister Roberta, I was too young to know the details of Mom's untimely visit…that she heard Daddy was going to split us up into different homes. A couple of social workers came to Daddy's house and held a meeting in the living room to discuss the matter of physical custody.

After some lengthy discussions between Mom and Dad, the social workers asked Roberta "Who do you want to live with your mother or your father?" That was a tremendous burden to place on a seven year old, but after hesitating a few minutes Roberta responded "Momma. I want to live with Momma." The social workers looked at me next for my response to the same question. Not that I didn't want to be with my daddy or even that I knew my mother that well, but I wanted to be with Roberta wherever she went, so I answered likewise.

Before the evening ended, all four of us girls (ages 2-7) left Daddy's house in tears as we were crammed into my mother's boyfriend's car and headed for Cleveland, Ohio. As I got in the car I looked back and saw that Daddy was standing on the porch crying too. I was totally unaware the night that I kissed my father goodbye that it would be five-six years before I would see or hear from him again.

## Journey Through the Furnace

Leaving Daddy and the country environment in Franklin and moving to the city of Cleveland to live with a mother I didn't know was not a smooth transition. Daddy wasn't there to help me adjust. One day my daddy was in my life, the next day he was gone. I blamed myself because my decision to be with my mother led to the exclusion of my father from my life. To make matters worse, Mom lived with her boyfriend Keith, who took the place of my father without my consent.

Keith lived in a substandard small two bedroom apartment and the four of us girls shared one small bedroom. Mom and Keith argued and fought often. In the midst of the domestic violence my sisters and I learned to lock ourselves in our bedroom and crawl up on the bed holding onto each other with the covers over our heads to drown the sound of the banging, screams, and glass breaking on the other side of the door that were louder than our combined cries.

Mom struggled financially to take care of us. She had never finished high school and had no skills for the workplace. To earn income she did domestic work, when she could find it. Money was scarce so we received government assistance and were raised on government issued foods (canned meat, blocks of cheese, powdered milk, powdered eggs, etc.). We created our own toys (old tires and anything our creative minds could manufacture). For a social life we visited Mom's brothers and our cousins. We didn't take vacations or attend church.

Mom didn't have friends and neither did we. Mom and Keith believed "children should be seen and not heard," so we spent a lot of time playing outside with neighborhood children. Mom didn't allow us to go into other people's houses and didn't believe those children needed to enter into ours either. She was very restrictive and kept us close to the house.

I was afraid of Mom. She rarely expressed affection, did not exchange hugs and kisses, and focused way too much on discipline. Her words were usually stern, negative, and critical. A strict disciplinarian, she demanded her girls to "be perfect." We were constantly corrected for any misbehavior and if any one of us got into trouble then all four of us girls would get a beating (not spanking). It was the anger and extreme force in which she

## What's Wrong With Me?

struck us, the objects she chose to use, and the fact we had to remove all clothing before the beatings – since she didn't "beat clothes". After my beatings I would have blood blisters on my arms and legs as a result of the blows from the belt or extension cord she used.

By the time I was eight years old, Mom had assigned unreasonable chores to help us become more responsible little girls. One of my chores was to help her wash clothes. We didn't own a washing machine so washing clothes meant loading them into the soapy water in the bathtub and scrubbing them with a metal scrub board, pushing the clothes up and down the board to clean them. On several occasions my little hands tried to push the clothes down the board but my knuckles slipped off the clothes and traveled down the metal board instead, badly skinning them. I cried from the pain and Mom looked at the scraped skin, poured some alcohol on it, and jokingly said with very little compassion "You'll be alright." I still had to continue washing clothes though the bleached water hurt my open sore. Mom was tough and she wanted her girls to be tough also.

My sisters and I took turns cleaning the kitchen. This involved washing, drying and putting away all the dishes, pots and pans, sweeping the floor, and taking out the trash. Everything was done to perfection since Mom was known for inspecting the dishes and if she found one dish that still had a residue of food on it, she would take every dish from the cupboard and make us wash everything. When my sisters and I cried over this, Mom threatened to beat us. We quickly silenced our cries but mumbled under our breath about the task set before us. Mom would fuss and sometimes beat us for being so careless, which taught me not to complain to her.

Mom was not mean and angry all the time. I would stare at my mother from behind the door and wish she would hold me and tell me that she loved me. There were a few times while my sisters were playing outdoors, Mom would call me from my room and let me watch her cook. There were rare occasions when we sat on the floor in the living room and watched television together. Those were the times I felt close to my mother. If Keith wasn't home or we didn't cause her any problems, things were okay.

But with four children, someone was usually out of line and therefore we got a lot of beatings.

Mom seldom talked to us about our behavior or corrected us in any other manner than beatings and spending time in the bedroom (nothing there but two beds and a dresser). For my siblings it was a terrible punishment, but not for me. I learned to be "a good girl" to earn my mother's approval. I was very shy and didn't like disagreements or fights so I didn't like playing with the other children for very long. I often resorted to my small bedroom where I could play by myself. I missed my father. I missed Franklin. I missed Lady.

## "Dirty" Secret

Little did I know that my void and desire for love and affection would cause me to be vulnerable to sexual abuse. Although Keith was in the house he had very little conversation with us. I enjoyed visiting our uncles, Mom's brothers, and playing with our cousins. But we had one Uncle I didn't like visiting. I don't know if Uncle Cool was related to Keith or just earned the title "Uncle" because he was Keith's friend but Mom felt comfortable leaving us in his care when she had appointments to keep.

At age eight, I had established quite a friendship with Uncle Cool never suspecting that it would lead to me being sexually abused. One day while left in his care, the other children went outside to play and I played alone on the stairwell of Uncle Cool's apartment complex. I usually played quietly outside away from the other children since I wasn't a team player. Uncle would motion for me to come into the house and watch television with him, allowing me to select the program. He gave me desserts the other children were not privileged to and treated me very nice. We talked about things that interested me, which no one else in my life took the time to do.

At first it was fun to have a secret. Then Uncle started touching my private parts and forcing me to touch his. This happened each time we were alone. Even though I didn't want to, I found myself submitting to his authority. There were several times that I stayed outside and watched the other children play to avoid being alone with him. He found a reason to call me into his apartment or motion for me to go to a door which led down into the basement where he would molest me.

I was too afraid to tell Uncle to stop, or scream for help, or even to push him away and run. I didn't want the other children to hear me and tell my mother. When he said "Come here" I went and allowed him to do whatever he wanted. All the time I felt dirty and ashamed. I didn't want him to touch me but oddly enough it felt good. I was confused. I was also angry with myself for allowing him to do this to me and for being too scared to tell Mom.

My fears bought my silence and covered his crime as I continued to live in fear that someone would find out what was going on. Telling my mother about the abuse was not an option I considered since Mom's extreme measures of discipline had me terrified. I was more afraid of what Mom would do to me than of the abuse I received from Uncle. Because of my silence Uncle became very comfortable with molesting me, which was evidenced on my ninth birthday when he came to our house to bring me a birthday present. That was unusual since my sisters and I didn't get presents for our birthdays. We had very little money so birthday parties and gifts were not something Mom considered a necessity.

Mom wasn't home when Uncle Cool arrived but my three sisters were there. Unfortunately their presence didn't prevent Uncle from leading me into the small bedroom I shared with my three sisters. He closed the door and pressed his foot against it while he fondled me. His play was interrupted when my older sister Roberta banged on the door. She asked why she couldn't open the door. He cautiously opened the door to see who else was there, and nervously said "I just needed to give your sister something special for her birthday."

That night I was terrified that Mom would find out about my "dirty secret" when she saw the present Uncle bought me, a box of checkers, and questioned me about them. I was so scared of what Mom would do to me that I didn't give much thought to what would happen to Uncle if someone found out. Even though he didn't threaten to hurt me or my family, Uncle did say that "we" would get in a lot of trouble if I ever told anyone our secret.

The molestation continued for two years until a family crisis happened causing my mother to uproot us four girls and my baby brother and move us from Cleveland to live with my maternal grandmother in Norfolk, Virginia. The move to Virginia ended the sexual abuse from Uncle. I was so fortunate my surroundings changed - but I was still a victim.

## Suffer in Silence

We arrived at Grandma Brown's to find out there would be nine of us piled up into her small three bedroom bricked ranch-styled home. My aunt and her daughter were living with Grandma Brown before my mother showed up with all five of her children. Mom only stayed at Grandma's a few short weeks before taking my baby brother and returning to Keith in Cleveland, leaving Grandma Brown to care for four emotionally troubled granddaughters.

Grandma Brown, like Mom, gave us chores and fussed a lot when we didn't do a good job. She made many negative comments but she didn't resort to violence or beating us all the time. When she did correct us, spankings weren't her first option. Grandma Brown wasn't affectionate and didn't hug or kiss us, but she was a Christian and took us to church. She did other nice things for us like taking us to the movies on Saturdays or taking us to the play park. It was through my grandmother's kindness that we were fortunate to experience a better life.

After living with Grandma for a while, my world was shattered again. I was given the opportunity to earn a few dollars cleaning the home of one of Grandma's neighbors. The neighbor was a single male living alone and needed some light housework done. Roberta usually cleaned his house but this particular day she was unable to do it, so I agreed to clean for her. Although we were young, Mom and Grandma Brown had taught us to do an excellent job at housework plus we were a source of cheap labor.

# What's Wrong With Me?

I did some light cleaning to the neighbor's house and everything went well until it was time for him to pay me. He was pleased with the cleaning and asked me to get his wallet from his bedroom dresser drawer. As I pulled the drawer open and grabbed the wallet, suddenly I felt his presence behind me. Before I knew what was happening, he pushed me on his bed and dropped his heavy body on top of me. I tried but was unsuccessful in wiggling my small ten year old frame from under the strong body straddled across me. Since I was pinned down, he did everything but penetrate me. When he was finished, he gave me a few extra dollars, more than the amount he promised for cleaning, and politely thanked me for a job well done.

Walking back to Grandma's house, I felt violated, angry, scared, ashamed, and embarrassed. Again, I was too ashamed to tell anyone that something so horrible had happened to me. So again I kept quiet. I hid the extra money to avoid any questions. I never returned to that neighbor's house again and would walk an extra block to avoid even passing it.

Whenever I got permission I walked to the neighborhood park, a block in the opposite direction from this neighbor's house. There I spent hours on the swings – singing and daydreaming. Those were my most peaceful moments – away from everyone and where I could escape reality and the pain from life experiences.

I can't remember when I first created my own fantasy world but I became totally engaged in that world. Unfortunately my daydreaming became excessive and my grades in school suffered. I went from being an honor student to making Cs and Ds because I couldn't concentrate. Grandma had my vision checked and because I needed corrective lens she thought that was my problem. She worked closely with me to improve my grades. I kept my secret. I was so good at keeping secrets that Grandma never suspected I'd been sexually assaulted.

## Violence Breeds Violence

I didn't like myself very much and it seemed that no one else liked me either. From years of living with domestic violence, the physical abuse from the beatings I received even for things I didn't do, the sexual abuse by my uncle and the sexual assault by a neighbor, I harbored so much pent up anger. I felt that the only way to control my anger was to isolate myself, but having three sisters and a brother, I found that difficult to do. I tried to be good and stay out of trouble but that earned me the ridicule from my sisters as being "Miss Goody Two Shoes," implying I thought I was better than them. There was so much competition among us. We strived for attention even if it was negative.

The atmosphere around Grandma's house changed when Mom returned from Cleveland. The beatings started again although not as frequent as before. On Saturday nights when Grandma Brown attended her Eastern Star or church meetings and Mom went "out on the town," my younger siblings and I were left in Roberta's care. Of course, Roberta resented having to care for us so she turned her anger on us.

With no adult supervision, Saturday nights became fighting matches where we were unmerciful toward each other. Our fights were as violent as the ones we'd witnessed between Mom and Keith. On one occasion Roberta hit me in the head with Grandma's cast iron skillet. As I fell to the floor holding my head in excruciating pain, Roberta jumped on top of me, grabbed my hair, and continued to bang my head on the kitchen floor repeatedly while I screamed and almost passed out.

Controlling my negative emotions was almost impossible when my younger sisters were masters at pushing my buttons to get a reaction. One Saturday night while quietly shining my patent leather shoes for church on Sunday, my two younger sisters decided to annoy me as usual until I lost my temper. I picked up Grandma's steel ash tray from off the end table in the living room and threw it at my sister who hid behind the curtain covering the picture window. Just as the ash tray went flying through the air, I heard a voice warn "duck." She did. The ash tray, which I threw with such force that the curtain couldn't cushion it, broke the adjacent side window.

Another time I locked myself in the bathroom after Roberta beat me for trying to burn my two younger sisters with the iron because they kept chasing around the ironing board while I was trying to iron my Sunday clothes. The three of them were determined to get even with me although I pleaded with them to leave me alone. Sobbing, I had to hold my finger over the lock to keep it in place and them out. The list goes on and on. It didn't matter how nice the evening started, most Saturday nights that Grandma and Mom left us unattended ended with violence. But no matter how often my sisters and I fought each other or how awful the fights, we'd clean the house and put everything back in order before Mom and Grandma returned. We fought each other but did our best to protect one another from Mom's wrath.

## Tension Behind it All

The sibling violence continued almost weekly until Mom was finally approved to rent a place in the "projects" (low income housing). For the first time we had our own place; it would just be Mom, us girls, and my little brother. I expected that things were going to be better but was disappointed with Mom's new boyfriend continually in and out of our house.

I resented having another man in our lives but being the "good kid" I was, I tried to keep peace around the house and accepted the fact that he was going to be around and Mom's attention would be directed to him. Then Mom announced she was expecting another baby. Roberta resented it greatly since this would add more responsibility to her. The tension between her and Mom increased and so did the violence.

Roberta and I weren't very close but I admired that she was attractive and popular, which I wasn't. As a preteen I watched her actions and interactions with people and asked her questions about why she acted the way she did. That's when she told me she was raped by Keith and that was the reason we abruptly left Cleveland. When Roberta said that Mom chose her boyfriends over her children, I understood why there was so much animosity between the two of them and why Roberta took out her frustrations on us.

Mom continued to "party" and expect Roberta to care for us in her absence. Roberta defiantly declared "those kids ain't mine" and started hanging out late nights with her friends. She no longer felt a responsibility toward us so I became the "little mother "and watched over my younger siblings. I was thirteen years old, very irritable, fussy, bossy, and demanding just like Mom and Grandma. I was a perfectionist and took control of everything. When Mom was home, I was content to either resort to the privacy of my bedroom or to walk around the neighborhood for hours.

The experience of watching Mom and Roberta war as rivals was devastating for me. Unfortunately, I had no one to look up to or talk to about my life issues. No one in our family ever talked about the violence in our home or the cause of it. Nor did we talk about "sex." The only 'sex talks' I remember was Grandma Brown's saying "Keep your dress down and your legs closed." Mom was sexually active and Roberta followed her example but we still didn't talk about sex, female issues, or relationships. What I knew about sex was learned through my horrifying experiences with my abusers, which left me feeling dirty and defiled.

## *Whispers on My Journey*

***On my journey through the furnace
I heard a whisper –
"For as he (a man) thinks in his heart,
so is he."
Proverbs 23:7***

*My thoughts became self-fulfilling prophecies for my life. I thought I was a failure and I acted accordingly. I thought I was a victim, and I was victimized. I thought I was worthless, and I had no hope. I didn't dream of a future, I just existed.*

*I read a lot of books but never read the Bible. I thought you only read the Bible to help complete your homework for Sunday school – at least it was my perspective when I lived with Grandma Brown. After leaving her house we seldom went to church but I often thought about God. There were days when I walked for hours with my head hung down thinking "where is God?" If God was always watching us, could He really see what everyone was doing at every minute and know the thoughts of over a billion people on earth?" Then I wondered "How does God determine if you're good enough to go to heaven?" I wished I could go to heaven but I knew something was wrong with me. I was different from all the rest of the kids. I tried to be good but I wasn't very good.*

*Because of the physical abuse, sexual abuse, and sexual assault that happened to me I saw myself as 'damaged goods' that no one needed or cared about. I felt alone, unloved, and worthless. I would give anything for a sense of purpose in my life and someone to love me.*

*It was difficult to comprehend how an all knowing God could see my affliction and do nothing to stop it. It wasn't until later in life that I understood that God had a plan for my life and my sufferings would be used to bring glory to Him.*

CHAPTER 4

# Mothers Cry Too

At fourteen years old, I had preconceived ideas about mothers, and mine didn't meet up to my standards and expectations; so I resented her. I perceived she was in her own world and oblivious to mine. Mom seemed more interested in her relationships with men and finding love than helping me focus on my future. As a teen, I longed for my mother's approval and prided myself on making good grades so she would affirm me - and she did.

My accomplishments and the positive remarks I received made me feel good about myself and motivated me to continue pressing for academic success in the face of opposition. As long as I made good grades and didn't cause my mother any problems I was considered "a good kid." However, I couldn't rise above the inferiority complex that caused me to be shy and insecure. I struggled with relationships and needed direction for my life.

## Too Young for Marriage
The summer prior to ninth grade, I wasn't social so I wasn't involved in any youth programs and not old enough for a summer job. I managed to earn some cash from a few babysitting jobs. Other than that I sat around the house bored and watching my younger siblings. I wasn't interested in boys or dating and had only made one friend, Terry. We met at school and I discovered she lived around the corner from me. On my long walks around the neighborhood, I would stop at her house. As we became friends, she

invited me to go to church with her. I did on occasion, but I wasn't really interested at that point.

While I was a "loner," my two younger sisters were extroverts and knew most of the kids in the neighborhood. One day they came home with ice cream and I knew they didn't have any money. When I questioned how they got the ice cream, they replied "Sheila's cousin bought it for us." I was livid because they were taught not to accept gifts from strangers. Sheila lived directly in front of our house and because they knew Sheila, they didn't consider her cousin Richard a stranger and proceeded to introduce us.

Richard was a very polite and kindhearted person. He loved children and would buy goodies for the neighborhood kids. For several days I stared out my living room window watching Richard's interaction with people, especially the kids. The kids loved him and the adults spoke highly of him too. He was respectful, mannerly, and didn't mind running errands for the older people (not the normal attitude of the young men I knew).

Richard had a part-time job and every day he would stand outside his aunt's front door, dressed in his work uniform, watching the children play and encouraging them to get along with one another. His behavior attracted my attention because he wasn't drinking and partying like other young men I had seen.

Richard and I soon became good friends. He was the first person who seemed genuinely interested in talking to me, in getting to know me. The depth of our conversation rapidly increased as we shared stories about our past and dreams for the future. We both had experienced a hard life. Richard shared with me how he watched his father die at eight years of age. He dropped out of school at age 16 to financially support his ailing mother and five younger siblings. After his mother died, Richard's siblings had gone to stay with his older brother in New Jersey and Richard took this opportunity to 'find himself.' Leaving North Carolina and not knowing where else to go, he decided to come to Virginia and stay with his aunt to see if he could establish himself in Norfolk.

When I discovered that Richard was eight years my senior, it didn't seem to matter to either of us. We seemed right for each other. Even

Journey Through the Furnace

though my mother and her boyfriend thought it strange that a twenty-two year old man was interested in talking to me, neither of them objected since Richard was so nice and we always stood in front of the house when we talked. Mom was glad to see me happy.

Two months into our friendship, Richard received his draft notice for the U.S. Army and a few weeks after that, he was gone. When Richard left for Boot Camp I was brokenhearted. I cried so much I didn't think there were any more tears left in me. I felt like I did the day I said goodbye to my father…empty and sad. After completing Boot Camp, Richard wrote my mother and asked for permission to correspond with me. She was so impressed with him that she answered in the affirmative. We wrote each other every day until he returned home on leave. Mom couldn't believe we had so much to talk about or imagine what we were talking about. Curiosity was killing her.

She proceeded to steam open my letters, read them, and try to reseal them before I came home from school. This became a source of contention between us because she never asked me to share with her what we talked about and I hadn't given her reason not to trust me. I perceived her actions as an invasion of my privacy and a lack of trust. Nevertheless, Mom was supportive of our friendship and welcomed Richard when he came home on liberty.

Richard and I got to know each other pretty well and continued writing after Richard went to his training command, then to his duty station, and finally to Vietnam. I shared with Richard my success in school because his approval meant everything to me.

In his letters Richard always encouraged me, told me how smart I was, and how much he believed in me. I was so proud of him too. In each letter I looked forward to reading about his Army experiences and the war in Vietnam. For years I had missed the love and attention of my father and being with Richard met that need.

I couldn't talk to Mom about my feelings, but there were two teachers at school I talked to. Ironically these two teachers taught my favorite subjects, Math and Science. They challenged me to take advantage of opportunities to succeed and always give my best to whatever I sought to do. Both were an inspiration to me and emphasized the importance of education. They pushed me out of my comfort zone, tutored me, and befriended me. I felt privileged to have someone whom I could talk to about the things that mattered most to me, my education and Richard.

When I told them Richard and I were in love and wanted to get married when he returned home from Vietnam, Mrs. Greene, my science teacher, shockingly looked at me and said "Are you crazy? Is your mother going to allow you to get married? Girl, you are too young for that! Why don't you wait until you graduate from high school and if you still love him, then get married." Mrs. Briley, my math teacher, was intrigued that I was serious about such things. I tried my best to convince them that by the time Richard returned home I would be sixteen and mature enough for marriage. After all, I loved Richard and was good at domestic chores, cooking, and raising kids. I thought that was the criteria for a successful marriage.

While Richard was in Vietnam, he and I discussed getting married if he made it home from the war. He sent his money to me and I opened up a bank account and faithfully saved the money so we would have something for our future. Richard made it home from the war but he wasn't the same person as he was before he left. The war had changed him. However, we were in love and pursued marriage. Richard got my mother's consent but he didn't want to set a date until he found employment. As a Vietnam veteran he had difficulty finding employment and it took several months before he found a job. By that time, Richard had exhausted all our savings on his living expenses.

Tension grew between Mom and Richard and he demanded we slip away to the Justice of the Peace to marry. After we paid the fees for the marriage, we only had seven dollars left in our savings account. I left the courthouse feeling cheated that my family wasn't invited to witness our marriage, worried about where we were going to live, and scared of Mom's wrath once she found out that we were married and she wasn't invited.

As his sixteen year old bride, I suppressed my disappointment in order to keep peace and not upset Richard. I didn't want him to think that my family meant more to me than he did.

## Mama, Help Me Please

We had no money and nowhere to live after we eloped so we had to depend on Mom allowing us to stay with her for a while. I wasn't comfortable with our mother-daughter relationship before Richard came into my life, and being married only complicated matters. On one hand Mom wanted to know everything Richard and I were doing, and on the other hand Richard wanted to keep all our plans private. I was caught in the middle and it brought contention between all of us.

Some of the decisions Richard made were irrational and unreasonable at times, but I never addressed the problem with him or anyone else. I kept my feelings to myself because Richard was happy to have a wife and to make all the decisions for us. My respect for him slowly diminished as he continued to play "control and mind games" with me and my family.

Steering clear of Mom had worked in the past but now that I needed to talk to her I couldn't. We hadn't built a strong mother-daughter relationship. She made comments like "You're not a little girl anymore, you're a woman." I didn't know what it meant to be a woman or wife either for that matter. I didn't know what she expected of me or what Richard expected. Nevertheless, I tried to please them both. There was so much I didn't know about marriage and men. My relationship with Richard was my first real male-female relationship and I had no idea that my sexual abuse and sexual assault would have such a negative impact on our sexual relationship. I didn't know what was normal or not. I longed for intimacy but the sexual contact was something I struggled with. However, I was determined to fulfill my 'duties' as a wife, so I endured it.

I had so many questions but didn't feel comfortable talking to anyone about them. I noticed that Richard and I didn't think the same way nor did I agree with his spontaneous decisions. We'd only been staying with Mom for a couple of weeks when one day I came home from school and Richard met me at the street corner and said "Pack your things, we're leaving!" His decision was totally unexpected. I don't know what happened to push him into making that decision since we hadn't saved enough money for an apartment, but we left Mom's house and moved in with one of Richard's coworkers. I was shocked and couldn't believe Richard put me in a house with people I didn't know, especially with a man I had never met. I was terrified, but again I didn't share my feelings with Richard.

I didn't want to live in Mom's house, but I didn't want to move in with a couple and their six children either. The family was nice but gave us very little privacy. His wife tried to befriend me but I was uncomfortable living in her house. My own insecurities motivated me to find an apartment for us. Being extremely shy and not having any experience conducting business before, I accepted the first apartment the real estate agent showed me. The apartment was substandard, but affordable. We moved in, and I did I all I could to make it our home.

I continued with my studies at school. I was determined to graduate from high school in spite of being married. While the other seniors were dating, enjoying all the extracurricular activities associated with their senior year in high school, and preparing for college, I was at home with my husband preparing for our first child. Nevertheless, some of my teachers still encouraged me to go to college. Richard, however, had already started ridiculing me and frequently made derogatory remarks like "Since you're so smart" and "You know everything."

I knew if I wanted a good relationship with Richard that I couldn't pursue my dreams of becoming a teacher. It was obvious he was intimidated by my academic accomplishments. I wanted to do whatever I could to diminish his insecurities.

Graduation time arrived and I marched across the stage to receive my diploma - an honor student and seven months pregnant. Roberta had dropped out of school for a year to have a baby, so she and I graduated together. Because we marched in alphabetical order my big sister's name was called before mine, which was so appropriate. It was a grand occasion and not only my family members in Norfolk area attended, but my father came from North Carolina and my brother-in-law from New Jersey joined the celebration. Even though Roberta and I no longer lived with Mom, she was still the proud mother watching her two oldest daughters accomplish something she hadn't.

## Like My Mother

Two months after graduation I gave birth to our first child, Allison. Richard and I loved our beautiful baby girl and she was "daddy's pride and joy." We couldn't bear the thought of raising our child in that substandard apartment so we utilized Richard's veterans' benefits and purchased a home. We were thrilled. This was a major accomplishment for two young people who had grown up in poverty. Richard took great pride in providing for his family and worked many hours to pay the bills and other financial responsibilities. Eventually I got a job to lighten the financial burden on him.

Just when we began to prosper financially, I discovered I was expecting another child. It was so unexpected! Allison was only seventeen months old when I gave birth to our son Junior. Mom was always available whenever I went into labor to have my children, but after the babies were born and I was released from the hospital she was no longer engaged. I couldn't understand it. I needed her.

At age nineteen I was mother of two children, owned my own house, and drove the latest model car but I wasn't happy. Richard and I weren't spending time together like we used to. He became a workaholic and thought his only responsibility was providing our financial needs. Working outside the home, while raising an infant and a toddler, was overwhelming and draining for me. I often wished I could get some advice from Mom or have her help. I wanted my mother to hold me in her arms or let me cry on her shoulders. Life was hard, being a mother was challenging, and without a support system, I was lonely.

History has a way of repeating itself. After I became a mother, I found out that I was more like my mother than I realized. Like Mom, I married at sixteen, had my first child at seventeen, and had birthed two children by the time I was nineteen. Like Mom, I was starving for love and acceptance from a man. Mom was easily angered, very irritable, and pessimistic - finding fault in everything…so was I.

Of all my siblings, I'm the one with physical features like my mother. I was so much like my mother and often wanted to be someone other than myself. Why couldn't I be a woman that inspired her children and built up her husband's self-confidence? I dreamed of becoming that woman and struggled to make that dream a reality. But in spite of my desires, I found myself criticizing the actions of my children, fussing because they didn't do things right, and complaining about the task I had to accomplish alone. What I didn't want to become, I became (an image of my mom). And I resented it.

## *Whispers on My Journey*

*On my journey through the furnace
I heard a whisper –
"The wise woman builds her house, but the foolish pulls
it down with her hands."
Proverbs 14:1*

*For most of my life I focused on Mom's shortcomings. I was angry with her for the painful memories of my early childhood. I was angry that she couldn't see my pain because she was too preoccupied seeking her own happiness. I was angry that she put herself and her children into harmful and dangerous situations. I expected my mother to be an example for me, to protect me, to have my best interest at heart, and to prepare me so I could prosper in this world. It took years before I realized that in spite of the beatings I received as a child, the negative remarks directed at me, and the lack of affection, that my mother probably loved me the best she knew how and to the best of her ability.*

*What I didn't understand as I was growing up is that my mother was a person. She had unresolved issues and no one to turn to. She took on adult responsibilities too early. She was pregnant at sixteen and had to drop out of school. Maybe she was angry because she wasn't able to fulfill her dreams. She and my father got married because it was "the right thing to do." Mom had four girls, each less than two years apart. I can only speculate how my mother felt at twenty two years old, unprepared to take care of four children or how she felt being married to an unfaithful husband.*

*As a young adult, I could only see her hard outer shell. I wasn't aware of her emotional struggles because she never shared feelings about her past, disappointment over broken dreams, or fears about the uncertainty of life. She seemed detached and aloof. I never knew her as a woman. It seemed my mother had difficulty coping with life but I learned to appreciate the fact that she did what she thought was necessary to keep us together as a family.*

*Focusing on my mother's weaknesses wouldn't help me become the mother I wanted to be. All my problems were not directly due to my relationship with my mother, but it had a tremendous impact on how I valued myself and handled situations. I focused so much on her negative acts that I often forgot about the good times we had together. In spite of the many sacrifices she made, life wasn't pleasant for me as I was growing up. It became even more difficult when I stepped into an adult role. Being a good mother took more than time and energy; it required emotional stability. It was my responsibility to seek healing so I could raise healthy children and have the relationship with my children that I desperately desired.*

*Reading books gave me the knowledge I needed, but it didn't give me the will power to change my behavior. I tried to live up to my own expectations but often reverted back into the same pattern again and again which caused me to have the "woe is me" attitude. I couldn't help but wonder if this was the same struggle my mother encountered. I understood my limitations and knew I needed help.*

# Part II
# Heat in the Furnace

*The blacksmith cannot mold iron in its original form but must put heat to it to make it malleable. He watches the color of the heat to determine the workability of the iron. When the heat is dark red, the iron is becoming malleable. However, when the heat rises to extreme heat and becomes yellow, it signifies the iron is fully malleable. Only then is it adaptive to change.*

*The Master Blacksmith (God) knew how much heat or affliction was necessary to bring about a change in my life. He knew how much I could bear, even though I didn't. I often cried "Where is God in all of this? Why did He allow these things to happen to me?" I received no answers. Nevertheless, the Lord wanted to use the trauma in my life to make me a better person, not bitter because of the things that happened to me. In this journey, He would teach me to cry out to Him.*

*Change was beginning to take place.*

CHAPTER 5

# Lonely, But Not Alone

None of my relationships were going well. Besides my babysitter, I had no friends. My mother and I barely saw each other. My sisters and I had strayed away from one another and engaged in our own separate lives. All my attention was focused on my family. Though my two toddlers were the love of my life and I wanted the best for them, it was difficult to be the mother I'd dreamed of being. I felt inadequate for the task. My marriage was falling apart. Richard and I weren't going on road trips anymore and ceased doing the things we used to for entertainment and fun. His idea of showing love was to buy me things instead of talking and spending time together. I wanted him to be my "knight in shining armor" and bring happiness and fun into my lonely world, but he was looking for the same thing from me.

Richard was far from being my 'deliverer' and every day I became more aware of that. Unfortunately, neither of us realized just how emotionally unhealthy we were. I brought so many problems into our marriage but still hoped the relationship would bring the happiness I badly needed. Instead, it brought even more pain.

As problems in our marriage multiplied, over the years my feelings of inadequacy also increased. I knew I had problems to overcome but didn't realize the impact of Richard's unresolved issues. I longed for romance and intimacy but he wanted control; unfortunately, we both did. I tried to control my surroundings- to keep people from hurting me - and Richard wanted to possess me and the children. We were his property and he owned us. He harshly criticized me when I didn't do as he told me. For years I did whatever Richard wanted so he could be happy, but my life was so miserable. I didn't like being controlled. I lost my dreams and ambitions. I lost hope the situation would improve. Soon I just didn't care anymore.

## My Change

Within the first five years of our marriage Richard and I had accumulated nice material possessions, but in the midst of our prosperity Richard was unfaithful. There were no words to express the intense pain of my heart. My hostility toward him increased because he hurt me more than anyone else ever had. I loved him with all my heart, had given him my loyalty, and he betrayed me. Lies, hurt, pain, anger, and distrust escalated in our relationship.

All the anger inside me surfaced at the slightest provocation and expressed itself in arguments, slamming doors, shouting, and cursing. I had such high hopes for my family, but it was no different than the family I grew up in.

I didn't consider leaving Richard after I found out about his infidelity because I didn't want to subject my children to growing up without their father, as I had been forced to do. Still, raising a family and working a full time job emotionally drained me and there was little going on in my life that replenished me.

My lovely home, the nice material possessions I accumulated, and the good paying job didn't fill the void in my life. Nothing seemed to excite me and I was often depressed. I found myself just existing from one day until the next. Though I had "walked the aisle" at age eleven in response to a sermon about Nicodemus coming to Jesus and being baptized, I was still angry and empty. Even God seemed so far away.

I had one high school friend, Terry, and we drifted apart when I got married. One day for no apparent reason she showed up at my house. We chatted awhile and caught up on each other's lives. I was happy to learn that Terry was now married and had a son. I got excited thinking that our friendship would be rekindled but that wasn't Terry's intention. She had become a Christian and had evangelism on her mind.

# Journey Through the Furnace

For a couple of weeks Terry visited me and shared scriptures. I wanted to know about God but was intimidated by Terry's approach. She seemed demeaning towards me because I knew so little about the Bible. My wall went up and her efforts to convert me proved unsuccessful. After a few more visits, Terry sensed her visits were unwelcomed and stopped coming. A short while later our paths crossed in a department store. Terry asked if she and a friend could come to my house and talk. She was persistent and I was so desperate for friendship that I responded "yes". I really thought the three of us would enjoy a 'girls' evening together.

However, that Monday night was not what I expected. I peeked out the door and saw Terry and her friend coming with their Bibles. She introduced her friend, Joyce. They didn't waste any time getting down to business. The cookies and soda I purchased were on the kitchen table but I didn't get to serve them because the ladies were immersed in their agenda, quoting scriptures and reading passages from the Bible to show me that I was a "sinner". Bombarded with their questions I felt attacked… two against one. As the drilling continued my frustrations escalated. Whenever I tried to defend myself, they quoted even more scriptures. I became even more agitated when they said I was going to hell. I couldn't understand why God would send me to hell after all I had been through. I was furious!

Terry and Joyce began to tell me about God's love and how He sent Jesus to redeem us from our sins and bring us back to God. By that time, I didn't want to hear any more from them. With great indignation I shouted to the top of my voice "Get out of my house…get out now!" Terry looked a bit surprised because she had never seen that side of me. "Sure, but can we leave a gospel tract for you to read?" she asked and placed a paper on the table as she and Joyce proceeded to the front door.

Not bothering to walk them to the door, I went into the kitchen and glared at the cookies and soda untouched on the table. Grieved and disappointed by the events of the night, I turned off the kitchen light and went back into the living room. Reaching to turn off the light there also, I noticed the "gospel tract" Terry had left on the table. I picked it up and proceeded to my bedroom to read it.

Alone in my room, I read the gospel tract that explained everything Terry had tried to tell me about God's plan of salvation. For the first time in my life I realized what it meant to be a sinner and what the gospel was all about. My heart was throbbing as I continued to read about God's love and forgiveness through the redeeming blood of Jesus Christ. Before I finished reading the tract, I kneeled beside my bed and prayed the "Sinner's Prayer" word for word. When I got up off my knees, I was assured that Jesus had come into my life and forgiven me for all my sins as I asked Him to do.

This experience was quite different than what I experienced when I was baptized at eleven years old. This was the miracle of the new birth and a personal relationship with Christ. Immediately, I opened the drawer of my night stand and took out the Bible I purchased from a book club many years ago. As I located each scripture written in the gospel tract I highlighted it in my Bible. That night I fell asleep holding my Bible in my arms. For the first time in my life I was at peace.

## My Commitment

The week after I accepted the Lord as my Savior, I kept wondering what it would be like to go to church on Sunday. However, I was more concerned about Richard's reaction. Since he showed little interest in church and I didn't want to start an argument, I decided not to go. I was scared to tell Richard that I found God, too scared to share the greatest thing that ever happened to me.

The following week all I could think about was attending church so I did. Sunday morning I cooked breakfast, dressed for church, and quickly ran out the door. I told Richard where I was going but not giving him enough time to respond.

The service at Terry's church was the most exciting one I had ever attended. My heart 'raced' as the Word of God was preached with such enthusiasm and conviction. Everything the preacher said was interesting. Everyone in the congregation had a Bible and followed along with the preacher as he read. I wrote notes on my copy of the Sunday bulletin so I could read the passages again when I got home.

Immediately after church was dismissed, people gathered around to shake hands and hug one another. There was so much love there! I couldn't wait to tell Richard about my experience and invite him to come the next week. To my surprise and delight, Richard wanted to go. The following Sunday, for the first time ever, our family attended church. From that point on, the children and I faithfully attended Sunday services and Wednesday night Bible study. Richard didn't really commit himself. He wanted to come and go whenever it was convenient for him.

After I started attending church, the quality of my life improved. I had friends who worshipped together, helped each other memorize scripture, and prayed for one another. We socialized together with covered dish dinners, cookouts and picnics. Those were good times. I loved my church family, but I still didn't feel good about myself. Unresolved issues and negative thoughts still haunted me. In spite of all the affection expressed toward me, I felt so inadequate. I still wore a "mask' to cover my true feelings and hide my shame. Facing my troubled marriage, having feelings of inferiority, comparing myself to others, and yielding to pessimistic thinking often led me back to a depressed state of mind.

One night after completing my shift I came home as usual and put the children to bed. I don't know how the spirit of depression intensified to the point where I contemplated suicide. At approximately 1:00 a.m., I left my toddlers in bed and drove toward the Campostella Bridge in Norfolk with the idea of ending my 'double' life. The internal pain was too much to bear. As I was driving toward the bridge, I heard a small voice within asking "What are you doing?" It was so clear that it snapped me back into reality. I thought about my children, home alone. I wondered who would take care of them if I died and what kind of shame and pain would they encounter knowing their mother took her own life. Other questions bombarded my mind. "What would their lives be like growing up without their mother?" and "Would they hate me for what I did?" As those thoughts flooded my mind I realized I was being selfish, thinking only of my own pain. Bawling like a baby I made a U-turn and quickly drove back home.

When I arrived home, I was terrified at the thought of what I had done and how close I came to ending my life. I'd been depressed before but never to the point of suicide. I knew I needed to talk to someone so I called my pastor at 2:00 am. I shared with him what transpired that night. He demanded that I get my Bible and for over an hour he led me through the Psalms, reading one after another. He read for a while then he asked me to read aloud.

That night I had a new appreciation for God's word and the comfort found there. Holding the Bible close to my heart, I made a decision to "know" the Lord, not just about Him. I wanted an intimate relationship. Sitting on my bed in the wee hours of the morning, I committed to following Him wholeheartedly because He penetrated my self-induced world of isolation.

## *Whispers on My Journey*

***On my journey through the furnace
I heard a whisper –
"Those who are well have no need of a physician, but
those who are sick. I did not come to call the righteous,
but sinners to repentance."
Mark 2:17***

*Those were the words Jesus spoke to religious leaders who opposed Him eating with tax collectors and sinners. They thought they were better than other people. I had the opposite problem. I felt insecure and thought other people were better than me. I was emotionally and spiritually sick. I needed a physician. I had a void in my life and I was so glad that God sent someone to my house to share the gospel of Christ.*

*I was fully committed to being a disciple not a mere believer. It was important to read God's Word, but I also had to obey the teachings and principles He revealed to me. I kept reminding myself of God's love and the power of the gospel.*

*The Gospel in a Nutshell (John 3:16)*

*For God, the GREATEST Lover
So loved, The GREATEST degree
The world, the GREATEST company
That He gave, the GREATEST act,
His Only Begotten Son, the GREATEST gift
That whoever believes, the GREATEST simplicity
In Him, the GREATEST person
Should not perish, the GREATEST promise
But, the GREATEST difference
Have, the GREATEST certainty
Everlasting life, the GREATEST promise!*

*Author Unknown*

Lonely, But Not Alone

*The night I contemplated suicide wasn't my time to die. God wanted to teach me how to live. My new life in Christ started a chain reaction of changes that caused me to grow spiritually and put me on the path to emotional healing and wholeness. I had to let go of the 'victim's mentality' and learn to be grateful for the things I did have.*

CHAPTER 6

# A Family Affair

I was a Christian for eight years when Allison gave me the letter disclosing the incest. During those years, I learned to accept God's love for me. It had taken years, but I was finally able to look into the mirror and say "Sharron, God loves you and I do too." It sounded like a foolish thing to do, but it was a breakthrough for me.

Having found a purpose for my life and a reason to live, my desire was for my family to know the Lord also. My kids were young and readily accepted Christ but Richard struggled with his commitment. His commitment to Christianity resembled his commitment to our marriage…. one of convenience –"what can I get out of this without giving much." Nevertheless, I believed things would work out in our marriage if I remained faithful to God.

Twelve years in a troubled disturbing marriage where Richard had been unfaithful and even fathered a child outside our marriage, nevertheless, I did what I could to keep the marriage together. Growing up without my father to love and affirm me was devastating, and I was determined my children would know their father and he would be a part of their lives. I had hoped that we would grow to be great parents and raise healthy, happy children.

## Children Pain
I didn't think it strange when Richard agreed to help around the house and with the children while I took a few college classes in the evenings.

# A Family Affair

I was working a full time job but thought I could invest time in fulfilling my desire for a college education. When Allison complained that I wasn't spending enough time with her, I completed a couple semesters then put my education on hold again. I realized that raising a family, working a full time job, teaching Sunday school, and going to college in the evenings was just too much. My children were not getting enough of my undivided attention.

When I stopped taking college classes and began to spend more time at home, Richard and I could barely get along with one another. He wanted to come and go as he pleased with no accountability and I was getting to the point where I was glad when he wasn't around. We were living two different lifestyles, and I was unaware of the evil that had been birthed. Incest had happened.

Subsequent to reporting the incest, CPS took action and removed Richard from the home and banned any contact between him and all of our children. My two sons, Junior who was only seventeen months younger than Allison, and Jeremy age three, couldn't understand why their daddy couldn't come home or see them anymore. I knew exactly how they felt because communication between me and my father was abruptly discontinued when I was five years old, and I didn't understand it either. My sons didn't understand the dynamics of what was happening. They just knew one day they had a daddy and the next day he was suddenly gone… no communication at all.

The children and I were instructed to attend individual counseling sessions. Richard and I were ordered to attend group therapy as well. My counselor was great because I was ready to open up and talk to someone about my deepest feelings and the secrets I had kept for years. Unfortunately, my children didn't have the same experience with counseling. They compared their sessions to nightmares and didn't want to talk about the incest or our dysfunctional family. I forced them to attend because I knew it was best for them. The entire family was in emotional chaos but I couldn't fix it. Only God could straighten out the mess and I continually prayed for His guidance.

Allison desperately needed counseling to cope with the sexual abuse. She needed support and understanding and I needed patience dealing with her moods. She changed from a compliant child eager to please into a withdrawn young lady who gained weight and wasn't able to maintain her grades in school. It was difficult to communicate with her but I kept trying. Often times she shut herself in her room or got in her bed and pulled the covers over her head. Then at other times she wanted to be near me. It was an emotional roller coaster ride.

I wasn't the only one who noticed the change in Allison's behavior. One lady at church, Mrs. Betty, asked if Allison could spend the day with her. I will be forever grateful for the kindness she showed my daughter. She took her on a shopping spree and pampered Allison so she would know how special she was. Mrs. Betty said "When I was a child there was a lady who pampered me and she made me promise that one day I would do this for someone else." I never knew what Mrs. Betty went through as a child but I could tell that she empathized with Allison.

Allison was the one abused but she wasn't the only one in our house that was trying to cope with the incest. My two sons were hurting and acting out their frustrations. Junior was obstinate and "strong willed." Having constantly competed for his father's attention and approval, he was distraught that his father was absent from the home and blamed me and Allison for Richard's removal.

Junior took sibling rivalry to a new level, saying and doing hurtful things to Allison and Jeremy and being even more defiant than before. On one occasion I had given Junior a command to do something. He snapped at me and yelled "I don't have to listen to you." Before I realized what I was doing I had grabbed Junior by the throat with my left hand, slammed him into the wall and positioned my right hand to hit him. Before I struck him, I heard that little voice in my head say "Let him go."

Immediately I released Junior and ran into my bedroom where I fell on my knees and sobbed like a baby. That wasn't the kind of person I wanted to be. I didn't tolerate disrespect from my ten year old son, but my behavior was certainly inappropriate. My anger was out of control again and I

# A Family Affair

felt helpless. I wasn't throwing shoes, slamming doors, and yelling like I did in my earlier years, but that excessive anger and rage was still resident in me. The incident scared me because the discipline was so severe and it reminded me of how my mother disciplined us. I didn't want to follow that example. As a Christian I needed to exhibit godly character, not the actions of an abusive mother.

Jeremy didn't understand any of what was going on and clung to me most of the time. Every morning when I left him at daycare, he started whining and holding tightly to my clothes begging me not to leave him. Fortunately, there were people in the day care center that showered him with love. One morning the pastor of the church day care center called me into his office to ask what was happening in our family because he noticed the change in Jeremy's behavior. I was thankful he was concerned but felt uneasy and too shameful to talk about the incest. I just told him we were having problems at home. He assured me that he and his staff were available to help anyway they could – and they did!

Taking one day at a time was crucial. From one day to the next I didn't know what actions or reactions to expect from the children. I didn't know what emotions I would incur. Some days seemed "normal" and other days one of us would explode over some minor incident.

Prayer and praise were my stress relievers. I praised God in the midst of my trials, even through tears. There were times when I had to remind myself that God loved me and I rehearsed over and over again God's promise to never leave me or forsake me. That's what kept me going. As a result of my hardships, my faith grew stronger and I was convinced more than ever to allow God to orchestrate my life.

## Sisters Reveal Secrets

Originally, I hadn't planned to talk to my mother about Allison's abuse or all the trouble at home, but she heard some gossip and called me to confirm it. That opened the door for us to talk about my sexual abuse as well, the secret I had kept for twenty years. It was extremely difficult to generate a conversation about my feelings, but I needed to talk about it. Amazingly, when I talked to my mother I felt like a little child again hoping Mom would hold me in her arms and tell me everything was going to be alright. But she didn't respond with affection. She seemed perplexed. "Why didn't you tell me?" she asked. I didn't answer but thought to myself "What would she have done?" Twenty years later I still sought compassion but the entire discussion about Allison's sexual abuse and mine were only a casual conversation. Mom couldn't feel my pain and sorrow.

Attending counseling and dealing with my own child sexual abuse made it possible to talk to my sisters about the hurtful things we experienced in our childhood. When they found out about Allison's trauma, they were very supportive. The love of Christ had brought us close together and erased the pain of the violent behavior we had exhibited toward each other as children. Though we had survived the trauma of our childhood, there were deep scars.

Each of us had grown up with secrets and ignorant of the depth of the other sister's inner pain. Now we had opportunity to reveal the darkness of those childhood experiences and get a clearer picture of the damage that was inflicted on us individually and collectively.

We had a chance to discuss how the abusive conditions in which we grew up made all four of us vulnerable to being sexually abused. We began to understand some of the complexities of our dysfunction and how it impacted our relationships with our family and others.

### *Roberta told it.*
Roberta had been sexually assaulted repeatedly for two years. Her innocence was taken while living in Cleveland when Keith, my mother's live-in boyfriend, forced her to have intercourse with him. Roberta was only ten years old when the abuse began. Roberta tells her story:

> *"It happened the first time while my mother was in the hospital for a couple of days. After Mom returned home, the abuse continued on a weekly basis. Most of the time, Keith would take me out somewhere, supposedly*

# A Family Affair

> to do something for Mom. I would always try to get out of going but he insisted. Mom suspected something was wrong and one night she caught him in the room with me. Mom was strangely quiet and nothing was done for a while. A few months later I started my menstrual period and went to the school nurse afraid the bleeding was an internal injury caused by the abuse. I told the nurse about the sexual abuse and before I understood what was happening, Mom was relocating me and my sisters to live with Grandma Brown in Virginia!
>
> Though I was removed from the environment, I never saw my abuser punished. I lived with feelings of guilt and believing it was my fault our family was uprooted. Since Mom knew about the sexual abuse and allowed it to continue, I felt unloved…and at times Mom's actions certainly reaffirmed that. Although I received lots of attention, it was mostly negative. Tension between me and Mom was unbearable and I became the object of Mom's frustration and the brunt of her anger. She blamed me for all her problems and often told me she should have aborted me. Those words filled me with unbearable pain. I felt so unloved and unwanted-totally rejected. If my own mother didn't love me, who would? I became the true problem child, super rebellious, doing whatever I wanted regardless of the consequences. Even Grandma Brown didn't know how to handle me. I grew up believing I had to take care of myself because I couldn't expect anyone else to do it."

Mom wasn't able to deal with Roberta and beat her unmercifully, but Roberta refused to cry. On several occasions, I pleaded with Roberta to cry so Mom would stop beating her. Roberta was obstinate and later told me "I won't give her the satisfaction of seeing me cry". By age fifteen, Roberta was pregnant and dropped out of high school until the baby was born. The tension between Mom and Roberta subsided as Mom tried to offer her support to Roberta during her pregnancy and broken romance. Unfortunately, after Roberta's baby was born, the conflict between Roberta and Mom resumed. They were true rivals. So Roberta and her daughter left mom's house and came to live with Richard and I for a few months until she was able to support herself.

I don't know of anyone more resilient than Roberta. As a single teenage mom, at age sixteen she moved out on her own and completed high school. She was the first one in the family to get a college degree. She was determined to provide her daughter with a better life than the one she had been subjected to. But Roberta hadn't dealt with her internal pain. She was always having trouble with relationships and finances, sabotaging herself in both areas. Her life was characterized by "drama" and self-centeredness.

Roberta came to know Christ as Savior and regardless of her painful experiences she refused to allow situations to hold her down. After raising three girls, recovering from two divorces, and living through the sexual abuse of one of her own daughters, Roberta is in the process of healing and desires to live a victorious life. She also has a burden to help others know Christ and the power of a surrendered life in Him.

**Precious concealed it.**
While Roberta was pursuing a better life for herself and Richard and I were trying to make our marriage work, my younger two sisters Precious and Kay were still living at home with Mom. Precious, just fourteen months younger than me, was the "clown" of the family. She hated conflict and prided herself on bringing laughter to tense situations. She used humor to mask her real feelings until it was impossible to do so any longer. Precious carried her secret of sexual abuse for many years but wanted to reveal her story:

> *"My relationship with Mom unraveled in my teen years to the point I took her seriously when she threatened to have me committed to a psychiatric hospital. Mom was totally unaware I had been sexually assaulted by some boys in the neighborhood. I never wanted anyone to know what happened to me. Our mother-daughter relationship was never close and expecting compassion from her was unrealistic. So I talked to Roberta who contacted my absentee father, living in North Carolina, and asked*

# A Family Affair

*if I could stay with him and his new family. The grass looked greener on the other side, but it wasn't. I didn't find the love and comfort I desperately craved from Daddy. To make matters worse, while living in North Carolina I was molested.*

*I was looking for love and became sexually involved with my high school boyfriend in my senior year. He rejected me after I informed him I was pregnant with his child. Having been abused and rejected, after graduation from high school there was no reason for me to stay in North Carolina, so I returned to Norfolk and stayed with Roberta for a couple months. Richard and his brother introduced me to a friend of theirs and a few months before my baby was born, we married.*

*A few years later I gave my husband a daughter and another son. Having a family was very important but I still couldn't remove the mask that was hiding my feelings and insecurities. I never shared my secret of the sexual assault and molestation with anyone. I did my best to hide behind my self-made wall. I was an emotional pendulum, swinging back and forth from clowning to despondency. The stresses of the marriage relationship and the secrecy of the sexual assault and abuse took a huge toll on my mental and physical well-being."*

Precious began to have medical problems and after twelve years of marriage, it ended in divorce. Precious' medical conditions worsened and serious health problems diminished the quality of her life. However, in spite of the numerous surgeries and doctors giving up on her, Precious loved the Lord and knew He had a reason for keeping her alive. Even in the midst of her emotional and physical pain she took advantage of the opportunities to encourage others in their faith in God. She inspired and opened her heart to her nieces and nephews in their times of trouble.

It took years before Precious was able to talk to us (her three sisters) about her sexual abuse and assault. I remember the day she and I sat on her bed and talked about her past. I put my arms around her and she released the tears she successfully held back for many years. Then she said "I still feel like a little girl crying out for mom to help me."

At the writing of this book, Precious asked to include her story and tell everyone "child sexual abuse will destroy you and your relationships if you keep the secret bottled up inside and refuse to deal with it." Precious was dealing with the feelings she kept hid for years. After many years of suffering, we all grieved Precious' death. She'll be remembered for her relentless faith that impacted so many lives. We'll cherish the memories of a woman who was truly precious.

### *Kay hit the mute button.*

While Precious was in North Carolina with Daddy, Kay (the youngest of the four sisters) still lived with Mom. Kay had a highly explosive temper and very aggressive. Like Roberta, Kay was very self-willed. She was a fighter and didn't hesitate to throw punches to instill fear in others not to "mess" with her.

When Kay reached her teen years, the tension between her and Mom was intolerable. Kay was ready to leave home like the rest of us had done and the dysfunctional relationship helped make it happen. Kay was fourteen years old when she left home and tells her story:

> *"During one of my altercations with Mom, while she was beating me about some foolish infraction, I had a moment of "temporary insanity" and before I knew it I struck her back. In a flash I realized what I did. Dressed in a pair of shorts, tank top, and barefoot, I literally ran for my life. Mom had promised if we ever raised a hand to her she would kill us - and I definitely believed her. I looked behind me and saw Mom coming down the street with a "two by four". I knew my life was in danger.*
>
> *Hiding for hours in the bushes of one of Richard's friend's house, his mother found me and wanted to help. I sat in her living room and overheard her son talking to my brother-in-law, Richard, who was about to leave and make a delivery in North Carolina. After he finished his call, I asked if he would take me to my sister's house. Before we reached Sharron's house I got out at the corner where Richard's 18-wheeler truck was parked and hid in the sleeper. I had never been so scared in my life.*

## A Family Affair

*When Richard opened his door, I told him what happened and requested he take me to my dad in North Carolina.*

*I arrived at dad's house and Precious and I were so happy to be together again. Sad to say, that joy was only for a moment. I heard my stepmother tell my dad "Oh no! Not here. We already have one. We can't take another and especially not Kay, she has to go back. I'm sorry but I just can't take two of them." The pain of being rejected from my dad was overwhelming and my tears were like an ocean coming from my eyes.*

*After Richard made his delivery he came back to Dad's house to get me. I knew I couldn't go to Mom's so Richard and Sharron agreed to let me live with them. Living with my sister, just three years older than me and raising her own child, I could hardly say she was raising me. She did however provide a place for me to stay and rules to obey while living in her home. I stayed with them for two years and had adjusted to the move, was doing well in school, and thought things were going as well as could be expected. Then one night I was sexually abused by someone I knew very well. I didn't say anything the night it happened, but the next day during a family dispute, I exploded as I told Sharron what happened to me. She didn't believe it was sexual abuse and blamed me for it happening. Because the man was married, she accused me of trying to breakup someone's home. It was obvious she didn't know what to do or how to handle the situation. I was disappointed in her because I expected her to do something to the person that molested me. She didn't do anything and as time went on I grew more angry and resentful that no one cared that I had been sexually abused. I was scared, hurting, ashamed, and felt guilty it was my fault.*

*I started dating Richard's younger brother which added to the friction in the home. Things grew tense around Sharron's house and after a while I knew I needed to find somewhere else to live. So Sharron called Roberta to take me into her home and I stayed there until my senior year of high school. Roberta had her hands full with her child, going to college, and juggling a fragile relationship. I wanted stability and a home of my own.*

*At age seventeen Richard's brother and I got married a few months before my high school graduation.*

*Although I had a wonderful husband who knew about the sexual abuse before we married, I still couldn't share my feelings because it was too painful and shameful. I was a prisoner within myself. I stifled my emotions the best I could. However, there were times when my behavior was explosive but I didn't understand why. Years passed and I gave birth to two beautiful children. I found myself constantly fussing and having strict control over my children's lives. My desire was to give them a better life than I experienced.*

*For ten years I was frequently in the presence of my abuser and pretended as if nothing ever happened. I carried my pain alone. It wasn't until Sharron reported Allison's sexual abuse that I was able to tell her and my husband how I felt about what happened to me." Sharron finally believed me and I felt released from my prison. I was free at last!"*

When Kay told me about her sexual abuse, I was seventeen years old. Unfortunately, at that time in my life, I didn't believe Kay was sexually abused because her behavior with her perpetrator resembled a close friendship. I regret not knowing that some offenders befriend their victims before sexually abusing them. It wasn't until I reported Allison's sexual abuse that Kay and I were able to discuss how she was "set up" to be abused and how my unbelief intensified her pain. I begged for Kay's forgiveness for the additional harm I caused for blaming her.

Kay opened her heart and shared her feelings which helped me be more supportive to Allison. Through the whole ordeal with Richard's arrest, trial, and sentencing, Kay was by my side. It was a healing process for her as well since I never sought justice for her sexual abuse. Kay was finally able to deal with some of the aftermath. She and Richard's brother have been married for thirty-five years. She is a preacher's wife and genuinely cares for hurting people. She has a special passion for mentoring women.

A Family Affair

## Family Prayer

Life wasn't easy for the four of us girls and we all dealt with our pain differently. Roberta was rebellious, I was shy and isolated, Precious clowned around and joked a lot, and Kay was a fighter. We made it through those childhood and early adult years and moved toward our healing. I give honor to my three godly grandparents who knew the power of intercessory prayer. Although they weren't part of our daily lives and were unaware of all the sexual abuse going on, they prayed that the Lord would watch over us and draw us to Himself. And over time He did. For the short time we stayed with Grandma Brown, she planted a seed of faith in our lives as she sat us in front of the television to listen to Billy Graham Crusades. It seemed we never missed a viewing of the program.

My paternal grandparents had very little access to us while we were children but the few times we stayed with them we experienced peace and love in their home. Granddaddy, better known as Bishop Martin by his denomination, was confined to a wheelchair. When he was thirty five years old he was doing some roof repair and fell from the roof and landed flat on his back causing him to be paralyzed from the waist down. Our grandmother was a woman of faith, a wonderful wife, and full of love. She doted on and cared for Granddaddy for forty-eight years until the day she died. My sisters and I were young when we visited with them, but remember mocking how they constantly called each other "Doll" and "Babe" and respected each other.

It wasn't until I became a Christian that I spent time with my grandparents and witnessed the depth of Granddaddy's faith and love for God. My grandfather was limited in his ability to get around but he was unconfined in his faith. For years he interceded on our behalf and expected great things from God. He had confidence in God and wasn't afraid of anything. I asked the Lord to give me faith like that man! Little did I know "that kind of fearless faith" comes only by way of obedience and praise during sufferings.

## *Whispers on My Journey*

***On my journey through the furnace
I heard a whisper –
"Silence isn't golden; sometimes it's just plain yellow (coward)."***

*That statement sounds rather harsh but it was true regarding child sexual abuse in our family. Because of fear some of us were silent. We were afraid to tell for fear of getting someone in trouble, fear of being punished, fear of being judged, fear of bringing harm to the family, fear of not being believed, and fear of whatever else. Even when it was disclosed, there was a lack of support for the victim who continued to live in fear of what others thought of them, fear of being hurt again, fear of betrayal, fear of not living up to expectations, fear of failure, fear of rejection, and the list goes on.*

*I sought for answers how my three sisters and I could be sexually abused by different men. What was it about us that made us vulnerable to the inappropriate attention? And how could my own daughter be abused and I not know it was happening. I didn't know the common thread that ran through our family that caused the sexual abuse to repeat to another generation. I didn't have all the answers but I knew that secrecy and not dealing with the crime was a major issue.*

*Incest and sexual abuse affected everyone in our family, not just the victim. The dysfunction itself caused turmoil and chaos. I can only imagine if sexual abuse was considered an illness or life threatening disease how differently we would have handled it. We wouldn't have been afraid to warn others about something that destroyed lives. Yet sexual abuse was destroying lives and passing from one generation to the next. It took years before we got the courage to address it. Research shows that some sexual abuse victims marry perpetrators and some become abusive parent and caretakers - physically, emotionally, or sexually, destroying more lives, homes, and communities.*

A Family Affair

*My grandparents prayed for us. I believe God answered their prayer and used our sufferings to draw us to Himself. We are all Christians and God is healing us, teaching us the value of relationships, and how to have healthy relationships. He has given us a desire to expose the evil of sexual abuse in our family and help prevent it from spreading to another generation.*

CHAPTER 7

# Whose Fault Is It?

Every time something happened in my life, I was so analytical trying to figure out who was at fault. Surely, someone was.

- Was I the one to blame?
- Was it my fault I was raised in such an abusive environment that made me vulnerable to sexual abuse?
- Whose fault was it that Uncle molested me?
- Was it my fault I was frail, friendless, and desperate for love?
- Was it my fault the sexual abuse continued because I was too afraid to tell anyone about it?
- Whose fault was it as a pre-teen my neighbor took liberties and sexually assaulted me when I only wanted to earn some spending money?
- Was it my fault my abusers went unpunished because I was too scared to tell my mother and grandmother about the abuse?
- Whose fault was it that I was so desperate for love that I married at sixteen years old?
- Was it really my fault Richard was unfaithful several times during our marriage?
- How about the incest, was that my fault too?

Richard blamed me for his incarceration, so I guess that was my fault also.

Whose Fault Is It?

## Blame Me

Blaming myself and/or others didn't resolve my problems. I was faced with real tough issues and I needed solutions. I had to admit that I wasn't always the victim. Some things that happened were my fault or at least caused by my decisions or actions. I owned up to my actions and put a plan in place to deal with them. However, I didn't want to take the blame for someone else's actions. I believed they had free will and were responsible for the decisions they made, like I was responsible for mine. I knew some of the problems in my relationships, especially my marriage, were caused by my inability to let down the invisible protective walls I built around myself. I didn't want to be hurt anymore yet the more I tried to protect myself, the more I got hurt.

Richard's unfaithfulness was like a knife driven into my heart. The pain wouldn't go away so I hid my feelings and proceeded with life. For years I blamed myself and thought if I had been a better wife and more sexually exciting then Richard wouldn't have gone outside the marriage for sex. Therefore his infidelity was my fault.

Through introspection and reflecting over my actions I tried to find answers to better understand how I contributed to Richard's damaging behavior. I had to admit that I stopped trusting and respecting Richard early in our relationship. As I acknowledged my growth, I knew I was far from being the innocent teenager he married - the one who totally trusted him and put such confidence in him because he showed love to and financially provided for me.

Over the years it became obvious to me that I was only "property" to Richard, to be controlled by him. He joked "You're my wife. I put a ring on your finger and that makes you mine." Unfortunately it didn't work the other way around. Richard often reminded me "You can't tell me what to do, I'm grown." That double standard created problems where Richard was not accountable to me or anyone else for his actions. He took pride in being a man- which meant two things: he financially provided the basic needs for his family and he could do whatever he wanted to do.

Meanwhile, I realized I wasn't the perfect wife either, although I really wanted to be. I was aware of my problems but I didn't know how to overcome them. From my childhood I slept fully clothed with covers over me regardless of the temperature. Sleeping that way made me feel protected so when I got married, I continued the habit. When I was naked for any length of time, I felt uncomfortable because I didn't like my body and didn't want anyone else to see it either. So many nights I wondered what was wrong with me that I didn't have much interest in sexual contact or activity. I wanted the intimacy but not necessarily to be fondled or to have a sexual relationship.

Early in our marriage I tried to talk to Richard about my feelings, but he was only interested in getting what he wanted. He was satisfied with having "sex" even though I struggled with being appreciated and attractive. So I learned to bear it. I didn't know that my child sexual abuse was the root cause of my sexual problems. I hadn't learned to appreciate the beauty of my body God created, so I covered it like it was something undesirable.

Since we never talked about my child sexual abuse neither of us were aware of the repercussions and impact it would have on our marriage relationship. I thought since Richard and I loved each other, we would be supportive of one another and committed to help each other. Therefore, the first time Richard was unfaithful I blamed myself because of my own sexual hang ups. But Richard's infidelity only exacerbated the problem. Although we stayed together and said we wanted the marriage to work, we didn't seek counseling nor did we discuss ways to "affair proof" our marriage. Richard's attitude was "I said I was sorry. And I'm not responsible for the way you feel." There were no signs of true repentance, only continual lies and deceit about his whereabouts and spending habits. It didn't help that Richard accused me of being overly suspicious of him. However, those suspicions proved to be warranted when I learned that he fathered a child outside our marriage, a little girl named Linda.

Having a child outside our marriage was devastating and crushed me emotionally in a way that took years to recover. Sometimes I blamed Richard for his indiscretions and at other times I blamed myself for staying in a relationship that was so unhealthy for both of us. I did it because I wanted to honor my marriage vows.

God showed favor toward me and placed two older women in my life that I could talk to. They encouraged me and shared their stories with me. Both of them lived through the early years of marriage where their husbands "sowed their wild oats" when they were young then settled down to be good family men after years of marriage. Unfortunately, the women never shared the hurt or pain they endured but looked on the bright side that they persevered and reaped the benefits. For me, the thought of staying married to someone unfaithful longer than I already had was depressive.

I admired those women. They were godly women who prayed for their husbands and showed God's love to them. Those women were faithful to God and had integrity in spite of their husband's lack of character. I made up my mind they had something I wanted…to be pleasing to God. I was determined that my actions would be right regardless of my circumstances.

I kept praying for Richard and praying for myself that I would be obedient to the scriptures so our home would be the Christian home I knew it should be. But the one area that really bothered me the most…sex, I couldn't talk about. I couldn't blame anyone for my inability to talk about the subject. I couldn't tell anyone how much I longed for intimacy but just got sex. So many times I felt "used." As I struggled in that area of our relationship, my insecurities only heightened after discovering that I was in competition with pornographic magazines tucked under the mattress.

With Richard's distorted view of sex and attitude toward me, I had to fight against the feelings of inadequacy and hopelessness that I would never measure up to what was "normal."

## Shame on You

For years I carried the blame for the infidelity, but I refused to blame myself for the incest. I learned that incest wasn't about sex but control and abuse of power - both of which were destroying our family. The incest was reported and Richard and I were ordered to participate in a group therapy session for parents who committed incest, along with their spouses.

The group was facilitated by a licensed therapist who allowed the conversations to flow freely. Each session started with a subject related to incest and everyone had a turn to talk. As the discussion progressed someone was usually on the "hot seat" for that night as members of the group focused on that person's issues. Richard and I were successful being quiet for a few weeks, but our turn soon arrived.

Richard hesitantly talked about his feelings for a while. Then the group looked at me expecting a response from me. I didn't even want to be there let alone participate in these grotesque discussions. Everyone had a sad story.

Maybe it didn't bother people to hear the descriptive acts of children being violated, but it bothered me. Equally repulsive was hearing perpetrators make excuses instead of taking responsibility for their actions. I'm sure the expression on my face reflected my true feelings. My thoughts were interrupted when the man across the room said "How about it, what's your story?"

As I proceeded to explain my feelings relative to our marriage and the events that led up to the incest, my anger towards my husband for his selfishness, and the pain he inflicted on our family, I was rudely interrupted by this same man who said "Lady I know what your problem is." Imagine my response…I thought to myself "You low life disgusting pedophile and you want to diagnose my problems." I'm so glad he couldn't read my mind. I immediately caught myself and silently prayed "Lord, help me to receive help no matter where it comes from. You've often spoken to me through others, so help me to hear the message this man is delivering."

> The man looked at me and continued with his comment
> *"Lady, you wanna be Richard's momma. You provide everything for him. You try to make his life comfortable. You choose what's right and wrong for him."* He went on and on then concluded with *"You've taken the place of his momma. He's not a man. He's your little boy. You control his life and he hates you for it."*

Whose Fault Is It?

*"What??"* I thought. As I sat there with hurt feelings and holding back tears, I pondered over his words. How could that be true? I thought to myself "Because I try to help Richard be a better person and hold him accountable, I'm accused of controlling his life and he hates me for it? So that's the excuse for his unfaithfulness and molesting our daughter!" That certainly didn't make a lot of sense to me.

I felt ashamed that night and left the meeting with mixed feelings of anger and guilt. As I drove home I couldn't dismiss that man's words from my mind. Needless to say, I was defensive and thought "how did this perpetrator become such an expert on my behavior?"

Not being able to make the connection between me having a control issue and Richard committing incest I asked myself "how did the sexual abuse end up being my fault? Did most people have the impression that I was an accomplice to the incest"?

The words that man spoke continued to echo in my mind and prevented me from sleeping well that night. Anything that bothered me that much must have some truth to it. So I rehearsed over and over in my mind the illustrations Richard shared with the group the previous night when he proclaimed that I was so controlling that he found it difficult to live with me. It was so interesting he could easily find fault with my actions when I handled everything around the house because he was so passive. I wanted the best for my family so I decided what needed to be done, and did it. I thought about the many times Richard was indecisive or extremely hesitant to do something so I took charge. I imagined that Richard perceived my actions, not as a help meet, but one disrespecting him and robbing him of his opportunity to be the leader in the home.

It took hours of pastoral counseling before I understood the concepts of codependency, enabling behavior, and being a "control freak." After careful examination of the facts, I agreed with the man in the group therapy session. I was a controlling person and Richard hated me for it.

Maybe Richard's extramarital affairs were his way of controlling his life, but why the incest? I still didn't have all the answers. Whatever his reasons he now had to face the consequences of his actions, and at last I wasn't trying to bail him out.

## *Whispers on My Journey*

**On my journey through the furnace**
**I heard a whisper –**
**"Rabbi, who sinned this man or his**
**parents that he was born blind?"**
**John 9:2**

*So often, like Jesus' disciples, I was looking to find the true cause for the injustices in my life and identify those negligent in preventing my sexual abuse. The sexual abuse, infidelity, and incest were all detestable sins that produced emotions of shame and guilt. Someone had taken advantage of me and my daughter and someone was to blame. Sometimes the decisions I made contributed to the situation and it was so hard to accept that my behavior was destructive to those I loved. If only I could turn the clock backwards and undo the damage, but I couldn't. Neither could I allow blame to distract me or sabotage my healing.*

*I owned up to my behavior that contributed to Allison being molested and asked for strength not to brood over my past behaviors, allow guilt to overwhelm me, or to waddle in self-pity. It was time for me to transform my thinking and concentrate on the future and not the events of the past.*

*In John 9, the man was born blind and it wasn't his fault or his parents. Nevertheless, he was in that condition. This scripture helped me see things from a new perspective. No matter how hopeless my condition seemed, it was an opportunity for God's work to be revealed. God takes the impossible situations to declare His glory. My situation was impossible so I knew I was a candidate for a miracle. For me, faith didn't rest in just believing in God's ability to do something, but in knowing He would do it - and that He would do it for me.*

# Part III
# Malleable for Shaping

*As the iron is heated through the various temperature levels, the blacksmith carefully watches to make sure the iron doesn't get too hot where it will weaken and simply crumble when hammered. Once the iron becomes malleable, the blacksmith easily shapes the iron into his intended masterpiece.*

*The Master Blacksmith (God) used my life experiences to make me malleable so He could shape my character. He began to hammer out the impurities in my life which caused me to focus on my own shortcomings instead of magnifying the faults of others. He began to mold me into a vessel to be used to minister to others with the comfort I received from Him. At times things got worse and worse, but during those times God gave me joy in the midst of my afflictions.*

CHAPTER 8

# Me, Love Him?

There's a vast difference in "being loved" and "feeling loved." My feelings changed so often, and I had to rely on the facts and not my feelings. For years I knew (mentally) that God loved me but I was struggling with my ability to "feel" loved. As I studied the scriptures I learned more about God's unconditional love – a love not based on my performance but on His own nature and character. The equation "God plus nothing equals love" helped me grasp this truth. What an amazing love! In my times of trouble I had to hold on to that truth. In my prayer time I cried out "Lord, I want to be like you. I want to love because you put love in me and not because I decided who is worthy of love." Those were great sounding words – and the Lord was about to use an incident to answer my prayer.

## Duty Not Love

Richard was serving one year in the local city jail with a ten year suspended sentence for molesting Allison. The boys wanted to see their father, so I took them to visit him in jail. After getting on the visitors list and waiting for almost an hour, our names were called and we were escorted to an area where several phones were attached to glass windows. The boys quickly ran to the phone and claimed their spot at the window. Shortly thereafter, Richard came out with a great big smile as he proceeded to pick up the phone and talk to his sons. But Allison stayed toward the back in the visiting room. I knew she wouldn't be happy to see him. But I had to make a

## Me, Love Him?

decision if it was better to leave her with someone else while the boys and I visited with Richard or bring her along as part of "the family."

I didn't want to give Allison the impression that our lives would just go on without her and also I didn't want her to feel left out or isolated from us. At the same time I didn't want to force her to talk to her dad. Allison's feelings mattered to me but I was just a little naïve not to realize it was premature for her to face her abuser. I clearly didn't understand that she wasn't visiting her father - she was actually visiting her abuser. I thought if she saw him behind bars she would know how powerful she was because she reported the abuse and didn't have to be afraid of him hurting her anymore.

As I visited Richard in jail, I thought he would appreciate the sacrifices I made to hold the family together. I thought he was grateful that I testified in court on his behalf (at his lawyer's request). Richard's lawyer knew Richard made many sacrifices working unpleasant jobs in undesirable environments just to make sure his family's basic needs were provided. He also knew Richard had unresolved issues from his childhood complicated by the traumatic memories from fighting a war in Vietnam. Trying to make the best case for Richard, he asked if I would testify to those facts. I wanted Richard to serve time in jail for what he did to Allison, and I also wanted the court to hear the whole truth about Richard so he could get the help he needed while he was incarcerated. Therefore, I agreed and testified.

After I testified in court, the Judge made a statement that insulted and belittled me –paraphrased as "this man molested your daughter and you have the audacity to come into my court and testify on his behalf?" The judge was right. I did have the audacity but it wasn't to avoid punishment; it was a plea to the court for help. Putting Richard behind bars wasn't going to stop him from being a child molester but maybe with some psychiatric help he could change his behavior after dealing with those hurts he had kept buried inside for years.

Somehow I thought a few months in jail and knowing he received a suspended sentence would make a difference. I thought Richard would admit he was wrong and that he had a stronghold he couldn't break by himself.

After a few months of taking the children to visit Richard, I decided it was time that I visited him alone. I made the mistake of thinking Richard and I could have a civil conversation about our children and how they were struggling with this whole issue of incest and daddy being in jail.

> Richard became confrontational and said *"You are the reason I'm in this place. You get mad when you can't get what you want. What kind of wife are you anyway to turn your husband in! You're supposed to be a Christian. Don't bother to come back here to see me again, I don't need you anyway!"*

He continued like that through the whole ordeal and not once did he acknowledge wrong or accept responsibility for what he did to Allison. On several occasions he even referred to Allison as "that girl" as he proceeded with his usual "It's your fault. You did this to me." His words were toxic, which caused me to question my motives for visiting him in the first place. I had my hands full supporting Allison and dealing with the children's pain and I didn't need to be subject to Richard's lack of remorse and ingratitude. I left the jail saying, "Enough is enough. I'm never coming back here again! He's on his own."

## Commanded to Love

My anger led to a bitter spirit where I had only evil thoughts about Richard. As far as I was concerned, Richard was worthless. It appeared to me that he had the mindset that whatever he did was okay regardless of who he hurt. He played the part of a victim, trying to get sympathy when he was really the villain. I'd been hurt enough and finally entertained the idea of not bringing the children to see him in hopes of shielding them from any future rejection. Because of the pain in my heart I wanted Richard to die – just go away forever. I didn't want to be the one to kill him because I could never take a person's life or harm anyone. So I prayed that God would remove Richard from this world however He chose. I was totally finished

## Me, Love Him?

with that man. I finally had enough and I didn't care about marriage vows, especially not "for better or worse."

The week after my visit with Richard, I was driving to work and proceeded to pray as usual. However, that particular morning nothing was normal. I couldn't pray. I tried but my mind was so focused on my anger against Richard that I began to sob and couldn't stop. I was still entertaining thoughts that maybe God would kill Richard. Although I had not verbalized my thoughts, God already knew them. That's when I cried out to the Lord and told Him what was on my heart. I felt used, abandoned, betrayed, and I hated Richard for it. As I prayed, the Lord began to speak to me in a way that changed my perspective of Him and the notion He would bring judgment when I wanted Him to.

That morning I "wrestled" with God. He spoke to my spirit and let me know that He loved Richard as much as He loved me. He hated the sin but still loved the person who committed the sin. But to me, the sin and the person were all wrapped up together… what he did was because of the person he was. I had categorized sin and child sexual abuse was at the top of the list. There was nothing worse than violating an innocent child. It was then that I had a clear revelation of Romans 5:8 "*But God demonstrates His own love toward us, in that while we were still sinners, Christ died for us.*"

The Lord reminded me again that His love was not based on performance or merit, and that applied to me as well as Richard. I knew that biblical truth but my heart wanted revenge. Richard had hurt me for years and then degenerated to violating my child in one of the most detestable ways possible.

Richard didn't deserve to live. Now God was telling me that He loved Richard as much as He loved me? I couldn't do anything but cry. God knew the intense pain and aching in my heart and could identify with what I was going through. He took that experience to teach me a valuable lesson. I heard Him say "I have commanded you to love Richard. I have put my love in you and you HAVE the power to love. " God reminded me that when I received Jesus Christ into my life, He gave me His love. It wasn't my option to love. He commanded me to love. Then I said "You are right

Lord. I have the power to love, but I don't have the desire to love Richard. I don't want to love him anymore."

Driving down the highway with warm tears streaming down my cheeks the Holy Spirit brought the scripture to my remembrance to *"love your enemies, bless those that curse you, do good to those who hate you, and pray for those who spitefully use you and persecute you."* (Matthew 5:44). I had no excuse not to love Richard, even if I considered him an enemy. I was called to live a supernatural life through the working of the Holy Spirit. His power was resident in me. I just had to die to my own desires and become obedient to His command.

Driving west on Interstate 64 near the Norfolk Airport Exit, I surrendered my total will to God and cried out:

*"Lord, please forgive me. If you want me to love Richard like you do, I need you to change my heart and my attitude. Take my focus off myself and my pain and help me to exercise my will to obey you and show mercy. Help me to see Richard as a soul for whom you died. Please, please help me Lord. Oh God, where would I be without your love and the mercy and grace you showed toward me? And all you're asking is that I show others the same love I received from you. Show me how to love and still stand against injustice. I want to have the victory."*

## Love is Action
The drive to work that morning was exceptionally long with the heavy traffic but I needed the additional time. I arrived at work with puffy eyes and a red nose from crying. But that didn't matter. My heart was rejoicing and I was worshipping the Lord for the special time we had together. I was clueless of the next step on my journey or the opportunities coming my way.

The next few days my prayers and focus were on having pleasing thoughts and controlling my emotions. To my surprise I had reached another level in my spiritual walk. I was overcoming the victim mentality by claiming my victory although I hadn't seen evidence of it yet. My

## Me, Love Him?

circumstances hadn't changed but my thought process was changing. Each time I had a negative thought about Richard I would quickly meditate on the encounter I had with God and recite a scripture.

Then it happened. Around 3:55 pm I was preparing to leave work when the phone rang and the caller identified herself as someone from DePaul Hospital Emergency Room. She informed me that Richard had a terrible accident and I needed to get there immediately. Startled by the call, I hung up without asking for details. I had no idea what was going on but I moved with urgency. Richard was still incarcerated but I didn't know his whereabouts since it was his first day participating in the jail's work release program. (The program was a blessing because the money Richard earned would help support the children).

When I arrived at DePaul Emergency Room they couldn't find any record of Richard's arrival. At first I thought I received a prank call. While the attendant checked the log to see if an ambulance or anyone else had brought Richard in, a man asked, *"Are you Richard's wife?"* I hesitantly responded *"yes"*, wondering who he was. General Manager of the warehouse where Richard had been assigned to work, he confirmed that Richard indeed had been brought into the emergency room. He told me that Richard was working on the roof at the warehouse when he slipped and fell through the skylight, falling 35feet before hitting the concrete floor. Several of his employees had witnessed the accident.

As I listened somewhat shocked, the doctor came to talk to me about Richard's condition. He wanted to warn me and prepare me for the sight I was about to see. In the examination room I saw Richard lying on the bed, his face extremely swollen like an over inflated ball ready to explode. His eyes were narrow slits that he could barely see through. Blood was all over his mouth and his teeth protruded through bleeding swollen lips. As tears rolled out the corner of the narrow opening of his eyes, Richard spoke in a quivering voice *"I told you I didn't need you, but I guess I do. I'm glad you came."* Tears welled in my own eyes as I stood looking at his broken body. Richard, barely able to move or talk, used all his strength to stretch his hand to touch mine. Then the medical staff took him to X-ray.

Hearing the news, Richard's brother came to the hospital. He assured me he would contact Richard's lawyer and take care of all the legal paperwork. Kay agreed to watch my children so I could remain at the hospital. I told the children their father had an accident, but I didn't share the details. We called several Christian friends and everyone began to pray. I sat in that waiting room for what seemed like hours. I reflected over the past few days when I wanted God to take Richard out of this world. As I sat there not knowing if he would live or die, I prayed for Richard's recovery. I didn't know if he was ready yet to meet God. Yet a part of me couldn't help but believe he was getting his due diligence for molesting Allison.

Later that night, I was informed that Richard had a fractured skull, several broken ribs, a broken right arm, a broken left wrist, injured legs, and broken teeth. He was rushed to surgery and had steel pins put in his right arm at the elbow and in his left wrist. He suffered severe injuries and it was a miracle that he wasn't paralyzed from the 35 foot fall onto concrete.

With the steel pin in his right elbow, a steel pin in his left wrist, and casts on both arms, Richard had to wear a double sling draped around his neck to support his limbs. He wasn't able to use his hands at all. He required total care for all his needs. That's when I heard a word from God. *"You're looking at my miracle. I want you to take care of him."* I didn't know what "take care of him" entailed but I knew I had been prepared for the task.

During the entire two months Richard spent in the hospital and rehabilitation, I served him not expecting anything in return. He seemed to genuinely appreciate my assistance. When Richard was released from the hospital, his physical injuries prevented him from returning back to Chesapeake City jail to serve the remainder of his sentence, but he wasn't approved to return home either. He was released in his brother's care and lived with his brother and Kay. At one time he was so independent that he didn't need anyone; now Richard was totally dependent on someone else for even his very basic personal needs. He was incapable of doing anything for himself. It was a humbling experience, especially since I was a major caregiver.

Me, Love Him?

I cooked and fed Richard and took care of his personal hygiene. During that time our conversations were casual because I wasn't trying to "fix" our marriage or "mend" the brokenness from the incest. I was there to serve and that's all I did. I prayed that during his emotional distress and physical weakness Richard would do some introspection concerning the actions that led him to this point. As he went through emotional ups and downs, I only hoped Richard would come to realize the emotional trauma the incest was causing Allison. As I saw him struggle from day to day trying to get back to what he considered "normal", I wondered what would be "normal" for Allison.

Allison was greatly disturbed that I was being so kind to Richard. I felt the need to share with her the encounter I had with God. I explained that although I didn't feel like showing love toward someone who had hurt us so badly, I fully intended to be obedient to the Lord because He has a reason for everything. Allison was still angry with God about the incest, and at twelve years old I didn't expect her to fully understand my actions either. She knew I loved her and I tried to reassure her often that I wasn't choosing her father over her. She was in for a long recovery process and I intended to be by her side through the whole ordeal as she learned the valuable lessons I was learning.

## *Whispers on My Journey*

*On my journey through the furnace
I heard a whisper –
"You shall love the Lord your God with all your heart,
with all your soul, with all your strength, and with all
your mind, and your neighbor as yourself."
Luke 10:27*

*Biblical teaching says if I love God, I would love my friends, those I considered my neighbors, and even my enemies. For me, to love others would cause me to die to my own selfish desires and feelings and be obedient to His commands.*

*I entertained evil thoughts toward those who abused me, especially toward my mother and Richard. However, my children were the love of my life and nothing they did changed it. I accepted it was my responsibility to love Allison. She was my child and the pain she was experiencing wasn't caused by her actions. So even when she was unlovely, it didn't change the way I felt about her. But learning to love my mother and Richard who were so abusive to me were my greatest challenges.*

*Serving Richard broke down the walls of pride I built around myself for protection. I didn't approve of his detestable actions and behavior and he failed at being the wonderful husband I desired so I struggled with even wanting to love someone like him. My negative thoughts and feelings were holding me in bondage.*

*My attitude toward God was displayed in the way I loved others. It was impossible to harbor bitterness and love at the same time. If I wanted to grow in my faith love was a decision I had to make. I chose to love.*

CHAPTER 9

# You're Forgiven

Richard had only served two months of his one year jail sentence due to the seriousness of his accident. His extensive injuries delayed him from returning to jail when he was released from the hospital. Almost five months passed before Richard reappeared before the court to hear the Judge declare that he had to return to Chesapeake City Jail to serve the remainder of his sentence. Because he was still unable to fully care for himself, another inmate, a trustee, was assigned to assist with Richard's care. Justice was served. I was not vindictive, but I was glad.

I had served Richard to the best of my ability and now I was relieved to turn those duties over to someone else. While I had been learning about real love I was also learning about biblical forgiveness. I learned that true love requires forgiveness; they go hand in hand. In all that Richard went through, he still didn't ask me or Allison to forgive him. Neither had I asked him to forgive me. I was learning the art of extending forgiveness but I had not fully forgiven Richard. I wanted to but I still struggled with my feelings. It was not only Richard, but all my abusers and everyone else that hurt me that I had to forgive.

## Commanded to Forgive

For years I had the wrong impression about forgiveness. I believed if I didn't forgive my abusers it gave me a sense of power over them. I was afraid if I did forgive them it negated the things they did to me and they wouldn't be held accountable for their actions. After all the terrible things my abusers did to me, how could I ever forgive them for messing up my life and causing me so much pain? They didn't deserve to be forgiven.

That's how I felt toward Richard for the infidelity and incest and all the pain he inflicted on me and my children. Even earlier in our marriage Richard would say the words "forgive me," without any remorse, and I would say "I forgive you" but would continue to harbor resentment towards him and bring up the offense again and again. Then Richard would say to me "You haven't forgiven me if you keep talking about it!" He believed that old adage "forgive and forget." Maybe he was right. But I couldn't forget.

Neither could I forget about my painful childhood experiences. I was twenty eight years old and still harboring resentment against my mother for physically and emotionally abusing me. She was in denial of her actions, so it was unlikely she would apologize or ask for forgiveness. Because my sisters and I were able to laugh about our childhood violence toward one another and I was able to hide my feelings of rejection, they probably didn't see a need to ask for forgiveness either. I hadn't seen my perpetrators who sexually abused and assaulted me since the incidents happened. Did I owe them forgiveness too? Was I really obligated to forgive when my offenders didn't ask for it?

At first it was difficult to embrace the concept of releasing the resentment I had toward my offenders or understanding how doing so would help me heal. One day I was meditating on a verse *"For if you forgive men their trespasses, your heavenly Father will also forgive you. But if you do not forgive men their trespasses, neither will your Father forgive your trespasses."* Matthew 6:14-15. That caused me to think "Let it go Sharron. Let go of the bitterness and anger so you can be free. God commanded you to love and forgive and not retaliate. Obey and forgive."

In forgiving, I accepted the fact that I wasn't condoning the actions of others or excusing their behavior. Nor was I reestablishing trust. I realized no matter how much I held on to unforgiveness, my abusers could never do enough to redeem themselves or erase the pain and wounds inflicted from their actions. Holding on to unforgiveness only stunted my ability to move forward and heal.

## It's a Process

There were friends in the church who forgave me for the thoughtless things I did to them and I appreciated it. I realized that no one deserved to be forgiven, not even me. As I taught the young people, I found it hard to tell them to forgive when I knew I wasn't practicing it in my own life. I finally decided the Lord had something great for me and an unforgiving spirit wasn't going to stand in the way of me receiving it.

I can't say I instantly forgave everyone who ever hurt me. It was a process. I made that decision knowing it was difficult to let go of the resentment which had been such an intricate part of my life. The first step in the process was fighting my own negative thoughts. I made a deliberate effort to cease from entertaining evil malicious thoughts about people. Every time the negative thoughts bombarded my mind, I replaced them by thinking of something to praise the Lord about. It took real discipline and I had to be intentional about it every day and all day. That's when I saw the real value of memorizing scripture and reflecting on God's promises. I was determined I wasn't going to spend the rest of my life angry at people who needed help and were spiritually and emotionally sick.

One day I heard someone suggest that writing a letter to the person that offended you would help. I wrote letters telling my abusers how I felt. That I was disappointed and angry they mistreated me instead of protecting me. I wrote that I felt rejected and insignificant because of the abuse. Through writing I was able to express the feelings I kept pinned up inside of me for years because I had no intention of sharing the letters with anyone. I prayed over the letters and discarded them in the trash. The writing was for my benefit only - to help me release the anger and resentment I held onto.

There were days I interceded for my abusers and called their name in prayer asking God to heal them. At first, I felt like a hypocrite because my words didn't seem real. They were just words with no conviction. It was hard to imagine something good happening to those who brought so much pain into my life. Nevertheless I continued to pray for them. The more I prayed the more sincere I became. After a while, I really wanted them to be healed of their diseases and delivered from the vices that kept them spiritually and emotionally bound into their own misery. It was a challenge but I was determined to be relieved of the heavy load of negativity that I carried.

Somewhere in the process I learned to forgive – I found out that forgiveness is an ongoing process. When I thought I had forgiven someone, something would happen and the memories would surface again. So time and time again, I engaged in exercising my will to forgive over my self-satisfaction to harbor resentment. Over time, I wasn't angry about unpleasant and hurtful situations or entertaining evil thoughts about my abusers. Through studying the scriptures and having a desire for obedience, I began to practice true forgiveness, whether my offenders asked for it or not. I still remembered the incidents, but there was no emotional pain or resentment associated with the remembrance.

I was more focused on the great things that were happening in my life. I was getting along better with the children. I was making friends. I got another promotion on my job. Unfortunately, my relationship with Richard hadn't changed much. But I wasn't worried about Richard. I knew my heart was right toward him. My children misconstrued my forgiveness as an act of loyalty to Richard. I couldn't control how they felt either. I stopped trying to "fix" other people; they had to give an account to God for themselves. But I was content. I found peace, love and forgiveness in my Christian life and I prayed that my abusers would find the same thing.

## Whispers on My Journey

*On my journey through the furnace*
*I heard a whisper –*
*"Father, forgive them for they do*
*not know what they do."*
*Luke 23:34*

Jesus spoke those words after being ridiculed, beaten, threatened, spit upon, abandoned, and nailed to a cross. He had a heart to forgive not only His friends, but His enemies. Jesus was my example.

When I tried to forgive, I found out that it wasn't as easy as I thought it would be. I can't say I instantly forgave everyone who ever hurt me. It was hard to believe that someone violated me and didn't know it. To me, they just didn't care. But that was their problem. I needed to be in the right relationship with God so nothing would hinder my prayers.

Whenever I asked God for His forgiveness for the wrongful things I did, He granted it to me, not because I deserved to be forgiven but because He is an awesome God full of love and mercy. That's the love God wanted me to have toward my abusers – to forgive them because I had a heart like His. I even had to tell God that I forgave Him, not because He did anything wrong or was in need of forgiveness. But I was angry with Him for not protecting me and for allowing so many afflictions to come into my life. Trusting and obeying God were my major concerns because that's where I saw my healing.

At times, my faith was not rational. But I knew the lessons I learned were the same lessons my children would encounter and as their mother, I planned to be a role model so I could encourage them during their difficult healing process. I knew if I really wanted to heal from the emotional damage and brokenness from abuse, I had to keep working through this process of forgiveness over and over again. So I made a decision to let it go and be free to receive all the blessings God had stored up for me.

CHAPTER 10

# Take Me Back!

Learning how to love and forgive were the keys to developing healthy relationships and mending broken relationships with my family members, coworkers, and people in the church. While Richard was incarcerated, I was focused on my emotional stability. Things were not always great but I was handling them better. After Richard served his one year jail sentenced which lasted over a two year period, we talked about mending our relationship and bringing our family back together.

At first I was hesitant about reconciliation but as I considered Richard's experience in jail, his endurance of the pain and injuries sustained from the 35 foot fall, the humbling process of having to depend on others to take care of him, his commitment to counseling sessions and his accountability to the justice system, I had no reason to suspect Richard wasn't sincere in his promise to do whatever was necessary to reunite our family.

Richard wanted another chance to be a father and husband and I wanted a family. I really thought we could work on our problems together. God had dealt with me and I knew He was dealing with Richard. He had spared Richard's life for a purpose. I thought it was so we could have a productive family.

In spite of the challenges, we were family and had to pull together. As I prayed about the situation, I was convinced it was time for Richard to return home even though I hadn't totally reestablished trust in him. I struggled with that but knew the boys needed their father and some stability at home. I was very concerned about Allison's feelings about her father's return. I was convinced it was time for her to face her father and address the issues head on so she could overcome this terrible tragedy. I believed the longer Allison avoided Richard, the longer she would continue to have unresolved problems and a bitter spirit. I believed that bitterness would destroy her emotionally it was just as damaging as the incest.

Because Allison was a Christian and I had taught her godly principles, I expected her to follow my example. Forgetting she was a teenager, I expected too much from her - too soon. When I asked Allison how she felt about her father returning home, she stated that she didn't like the thought of living in the same house with Richard but said, "*You have to do what you think is right.*" Considering Allison's feelings and my own convictions, I didn't want to make the decision for Richard's return based on emotion. I sought spiritual and legal counsel.

Several sources validated that Richard should return home. Pastor Roger, whom I well respected, said "*you've forgiven him so take him back.*" Professional counselors discussed our plans with us and assisted in requesting legal permission for Richard to return home…and the permission was granted. In 1984 it appeared to me that the Commonwealth of Virginia supported reuniting families after the incest was dealt with. That was also my understanding when Richard and I attended the group therapy session called "Parents United." These indicators reinforced the idea that Richard should come back home. In addition, Richard had a ten year suspended sentence and a couple of years on probation; that would keep him accountable I reasoned.

## My Predicament

Richard came home and was surprised that we didn't just pick up where we left off. Things were different. He had to readjust to living at home and relating differently to me and the children since I was instructed to establish some boundaries where the children would feel safe. That was one of the prerequisites before Richard was authorized to return home. In the process, Richard lost his ability to "control" the family through intimidation. Never again would we blindly follow him. I was more in control of things happening around the house and I made most of the rules to govern us. It was difficult giving any authority back to Richard since he hadn't regained my trust. These arrangements were not the normal we were used to, but they were critical to reunite the family.

In addition to adjusting to the change in family arrangements, Richard had to adjust to being a person with disabilities and identified as a pedophile. Where he used to take pride in financially providing for the family, Richard had to depend on disability payments because he hadn't fully recovered from the severe injuries two years prior. Richard was accustomed to manual labor, and not being able to perform the routine physical activities he once enjoyed was disturbing. I didn't realize how much additional stress this would have on the entire family. All this caused me to spend even more time than ever in praying for each member of the family and seeking guidance and strength for myself.

Richard and I had agreed to continue counseling after he returned home in order to get our marriage on track and create a stable environment for our children. With all the challenges, we needed the professional help to assist us in working through our multitude of issues. Richard didn't like talking to counselors and wasn't back in the home three to four months before he decided further counseling was unnecessary. He insisted that we could work things out together as a family without the embarrassment of telling our business to others. I was furious that he had reneged on our agreement. The insurmountable task before us was much too difficult to accomplish alone. We really needed the third party assistance.

I began to suspect that Richard only made promises in order to get back into the house, the house he felt entitled to live in. He played the game well and was very convincing, saying all the right things to me and the counselors. Although that bothered me, the thing that bothered me most was the testing of my faith. I believed that I followed the Lord's will for our family but the results were not what I expected. Nevertheless, I had to deal with the current situation because it wasn't an option to have Richard removed from the home again without evidence that the children were in danger.

Meanwhile I became the eyes and ears of the home. I paid attention to every detail. I wouldn't leave the children alone with Richard. At night, I would wake up when Richard turned over in bed or left the bedroom to go the bathroom or kitchen. I would listen to his movements and remain awake until he returned. Months went by and I was deprived of a full night's sleep. My disposition became irritable and fussy. The arguments between us increased. Not only was I having difficulty with Richard, his insecurities made it difficult for him to communicate with Allison who definitely hadn't forgiven him. She was struggling with low self-esteem and distrust. She was quiet and very compliant and I was just beginning to realize how much she resented her father being back in the house.

Allison stayed clear of Richard and likewise he avoided her as much as possible and whenever he had something to say to her, he usually "talked at her" in passing. Dinnertime was the one time the entire family sat together in the same room and after saying the blessing over the food, we chatted about the events of each other's day. Junior and Jeremy were glad to have their father at home but unfortunately Richard was preoccupied with his own condition.

Richard really needed someone to talk to but being a "loner" he kept his feelings bottled up inside. We didn't talk about our problems nor seek resolutions…and that scared me. Fear paralyzed my faith and once again I felt trapped. I wanted Richard to move out of the house, but he wasn't going anywhere since the courts had approved his return. I couldn't live this way. This was not what I expected. Fretting and worrying weren't working. I had to pursue other remedies.

## Where's the Trust

Turning to my pastor for counseling only added more fuel into the furnace since Richard was not receptive to any intervention. He wasn't receptive to disclosing what was happening in our family, so he withdrew even more. Fed up with the situation, I made a decision that I would move out of the house and find an apartment for me and the children. I longed for peace and contentment so much that I was willing to leave our single family ranch home situated in the middle of a cul-de-sac and move into a low income apartment complex that I could afford on my salary. I just wanted peace and quiet. After a few weeks of apartment hunting and being placed on waiting lists, I found a vacant apartment. The rental office accepted my application and non-refundable deposit for a three bedroom apartment. The prospect of having a place for just me and the children was exciting and lifted my spirits.

The day after I submitted my rental application, I received a call from the receptionist at the apartment rental office stating she was instructed by the office manager to return my non-refundable deposit because he was unable to rent the apartment to me. She provided several explanations over the phone, but none of them made sense to me. I was confused. So she explained it again to me. Now I was angry! My hopes were destroyed. I drove to their office and again asked the receptionist for an explanation. She was very nice and handed me the "non-refundable" deposit. I knew this incident was too bazaar and God had to behind it all. Then I was angry with God!

My drive back to the house was quiet as I refrained from listening to the radio, which was unusual for me. When I reached the driveway my tears began to flow. I ran straight into the bedroom and fell on my knees. "GOD, I AM SO ANGRY WITH YOU! I AM TRAPPED IN THIS TERRIBLE MARRIAGE AND I CAN'T GET OUT. I've subjected my children to this awful environment. This is too much!" I wept for a while pouring my heart out to God. Finally I conceded

> *"Dear Lord Jesus, I do love you. If you want me to stay in this marriage, please change me. Please change my attitude. Please change my focus. Right now I feel so deceived. I'm so tired of feeling like a failure. No matter what I do, it doesn't seem to be the right decision. I try so hard but things aren't working the way I expected and I'm very angry about it."*

Being honest with God was not a problem for me because He understood my thoughts even before I expressed them. I wanted to believe the situation was in the Lord's hands, but in reality I knew I was the one still trying to control the outcome. Finally I had to admit I had reservations about trusting the Lord in this area of my life.

After pouring out my heart to the Lord I got in the prostrate position and just worshipped Him for being the Almighty. It was a time of surrender when I didn't have words to express my feelings and just rocked from one side to another. It was one of those precious moments when I felt the presence of Lord fill the place. I was standing on holy ground. My situation hadn't changed, but I had a revelation that God would work things out. He would use my marriage relationship to bring me closer to Him because He was more interested in making me holy than my temporary happiness.

## Blessings Unfold

As I focused on my own personal growth and what I needed to do in my marriage, I decided to be a wife in every aspect of the word. Richard and I resumed marital relations. It was extremely difficult because of the incest, lack of romance and intimacy, and lack of trust in the relationship. I knew the Lord had called me to deny my own expectations and be intentional about obeying Him. He was helping me to be a godly person, not just someone who did good things. This was impossible to do without the Lord's help so I prayed that my mind wouldn't be bombarded with wicked thoughts or create any visualization of the incest.

I began working on my own weaknesses and attitudes: anger, ingratitude, fussiness, nagging, and complaining. These were traits I had possessed too long. I was determined to replace them with more positive traits so I could be a better mom to my children. I understood what Allison needed and I encouraged her and affirmed her as much as I knew how. Nurturing Allison taught me so much. She was so much like me in wanting to keep peace around the house. Usually she kept quiet and was compliant. However, when she tried to communicate with me, she found it difficult. Sometimes her words were harsh and inconsiderate as she expressed her feelings. Even though her tone was disrespectful, I tolerated it because she was doing her best to talk about a difficult situation. I wanted her to know that I cared.

If only I could make up for the pain she endured from the incest and having to deal with her father. Sometimes I couldn't understand the depth of her pain. Even though I was molested as a child, I didn't have to stay in the same house with my abuser and watch my mother carry on a relationship with him. I could only imagine the pain it caused Allison. I loved her so much and offered her my understanding, love, comfort, empathy, and protection. Those were my best efforts.

I accepted the fact our family was dysfunctional but knew God was working in us. It was still an unexpected shock when I found out that we were expecting our fourth child. Though it was a complete surprise the anticipation of a new baby brought excitement back into my life and our home. The children were so excited about the little baby growing inside me. They would rub my stomach and talk to the baby. Richard was all smiles and grins as he joked that he was still a "man." Throughout my entire pregnancy, family and friends showered so much love on me. During this time, I had a new perspective on life. My faith in God had been revitalized. I appreciated and was grateful for all the wonderful things happening in me and around me. Things were even getting better at home. Overall, life was good.

Things at church, however, were being shaken up. People I had considered my second family for over ten years were pulling away from each other. Many other problems had developed in the church that distracted me from worshipping there. There was such gross negativity and constant criticism going around that I even got caught up in it for a while. It was heartbreaking to see what was happening. It was through that church I developed positive relationships, enjoyed socialization, attended mission conferences, revivals, and bible studies. It was there that I had been introduced to a way of life that I loved. It was there that I served so faithfully. I tried to talk to Pastor Roger about my concerns but he responded, "Sharron, God did not call you to be the pastor of this church." He was right. I was trying to fix things again. I couldn't fix the problems in the church any more that I could fix the problems at home. I knew what I had to do. I loved the Lord too much to stay in a negative environment that exhibited such unchristian behavior.

In the sixth month of my pregnancy, I made a major decision for our family. After much prayer, soul searching, and confession, I believed I understood what I had to do. I submitted my resignation to the church and said goodbye to my Pastor and beloved friends. I cried like a baby because I was walking away from a place which had meant so much to me and people I dearly loved, but I believed God would lead us to a place of worship that focused on exalting Him and obeying His commandments; a place where my family could continue to grow spiritually and serve others. Though we maintained ties with some of the members at the old church, God blessed our efforts to find a new church home. It was like a breath of fresh air. The children were happy and even Richard was more faithful in attendance. No one there knew our family history. It was a new beginning for us.

## *Whispers on My Journey*

**On my journey through the furnace
I heard a whisper –
"Trust in the LORD with all your heart, and lean not to your own understanding; in all your ways acknowledge Him, and He shall direct your paths."
Proverbs 3:5-6**

*I didn't want to be characterized as a victim of sexual abuse. I was surviving and I still struggled with the issue of trust. It was difficult to open up again and allow myself to become vulnerable to be hurt again. I struggled with regaining trust in Richard and wondered if I was being foolish in allowing him to continue being a part of our lives. I wanted to trust him even though he had proven to be untrustworthy. I even struggled with trusting God and questioned the Lord's direction for my life. I finally realized I had to be honest with myself; I didn't trust God because He failed to protect my daughter from the sexual abuse. It was only after I admitted to God that I had trust issues that I was able to start working on the problem. If I couldn't trust God, I couldn't trust anyone.*

*I had confidence God was orchestrating my life. Learning that nothing could happen to me unless God permitted or allowed it really bothered me until I read the biblical account of a man named Joseph (Genesis 37, 39-50). At a young age, God had a calling on Joseph's life. Joseph was betrayed by those he loved, falsely accused, jailed on circumstantial evidence, remained in prison for years for a crime he didn't commit, and encountered broken promises made by those he helped. God was working out His purpose in Joseph's life but it didn't exempt Joseph from tragedies.*

*I asked "God, where were you when Joseph suffered for all those years?" The Bible said that God was with Joseph. God was with him when he served Potiphar. God blessed Joseph to be successful to the extent that all Potiphar's house was blessed for Joseph's sake. When Joseph was falsely accused of rape and put in prison, God was with Joseph and showed him mercy. Whatever Joseph did, he prospered. God finally revealed his purpose for Joseph's troubles through a series of events that led to saving the Israelites during the famine. Joseph trusted God although he had no idea of God's plan until God was ready to reveal it to him. Then he said to his brothers who betrayed him "but as for you, you meant evil against me; but God meant it for good, in order to bring it about as it is this day, to save many people alive." Genesis 50:20.*

*In reading about Joseph's life I realized that I may never fully understand the sovereignty of God or even His plan for my life. But I accepted the fact that God is always in control and therefore I could trust Him with the details of my life… for only He knows the plans He has for me. Committing my life to Him meant trusting Him and claiming His promises even when He didn't reveal His plan to me beforehand.*

# Part IV
# Magnificent Product

*I no longer considered myself a victim or survivor, but an overcomer. Through my furnace experience, I reached a place of healing. I embraced the truth that I was not an assembly line product that was mass produced. I am God's own hand-crafted work of art – an original masterpiece intended for a specific purpose. God gave me personality, gifts, abilities, skills, interests, talents, and even afflictions to be used in service to Him.*

*As I kept company with others who were living victorious lives, I determined to have the same kind of life. I was intentional about being free...free to be honest, free to trust again, free to be transparent, and free to be me.*

*My soul cried out like the psalmist: "For you, O God, have tested us; You have refined us as silver is refined...we went through fire and through water, but You brought us out to rich fulfillment." Psalm 66:10, 12b*

CHAPTER 11

# Oh No, Not Again!

During my pregnancy I spent days just praising God and counting my blessings of how much He blessed me. I remembered a time I didn't have any friends and now I had several friends. At one time I made less than minimum wage, and now I was middle management. I had good working relationships with my coworkers. I appreciated my coworkers and all the support they provided throughout my entire pregnancy while I worked my full-time job.

At the end of one particular workday, my contractions began as I was driving home. Once I arrived there I secretly timed them. As the contractions accelerated, I slipped into the bedroom and called my doctor. "This is your fourth child, so get to the hospital immediately, and I'll meet you there" I was told.

When I announced to the family that it was time for the baby to come, my entire household sprang into action. Allison scrambled to find the camera to take my last maternity picture before I walked out the door. Junior and Jeremy yelled and jumped up and down excited they would have a new baby soon. Richard grabbed the overnight bag, helped me into the car, and quickly drove to the emergency room. Everything happened so fast. By 8:00pm that night I had given birth to a beautiful girl we named Elizabeth. It was such a joyous occasion for all of us.

## Manifold Blessings

I took full advantage of the six weeks of maternity leave. I loved being home with my family and not having to work outside the home. I wished it could have stayed that way forever, but I had to return to work, we needed the income. Since Richard was still on disability, he volunteered to take care of Elizabeth so we could avoid the additional costs of a babysitter. At first I was hesitant about leaving my infant with him. I wasn't intimidated by or fearful of him anymore and had learned to establish healthy boundaries when it concerned Richard, but I still prayed diligently for God to give me wisdom.

God gave me peace in answer to my prayer so I had no further reservations. I just knew that Richard would not harm Elizabeth, neither sexually or physically. Allison was fifteen years old at the time and she couldn't understand why I would even consider leaving Elizabeth in Richard's care. She hadn't regained trust in Richard after the incest.

Richard didn't like being called "Mr. Mom", but he did an outstanding job taking care of Elizabeth and doing housework. He had many problems but bragged that his greatest asset was a praying wife, a godly woman willing to stand by him in spite of the shame and disgrace he caused. I considered it a high compliment that he could see evidence of my spiritual commitment. I knew that I was healing from all the past hurts and prayed for our entire family to be healed. The more I put my trust in God, the more I saw the need to wait on God's timing.

It wasn't long before we were all involved in our new church. Richard felt accepted and although he showed very little interest in studying the Bible or anything that required learning the scriptures, he volunteered to be the church's auto mechanic. He really had a special skill working with cars and buses and there wasn't anything he couldn't diagnose or fix. He was so happy to be needed. He also helped with the maintenance on cars belonging to church members who couldn't afford the expensive repair shops. In addition, he enjoyed working on Pastor Sander's car as well as some older associate pastors; he called it "his service to the Lord". While the men worked on cars and socialized, their wives, in return, would babysit Elizabeth. She quickly became a spoiled little baby that everybody loved. I was so glad that Richard was spending time with Christian men.

My prayers continued to be answered as I watched Allison participate in the youth choir and other teen activities. She was still insecure and needed a constant reminder not to compare herself to the success of others. Junior was a "social butterfly" and enjoyed being the clown of the group, though it frequently got him into trouble. He was very popular. Jeremy was gifted with an exceptional solo voice and loved to sing wherever he went. My children meant everything to me and seeing them actively involved in and enjoying church gave us some common interests.

When we were at church we put forward our best behavior, but a home we didn't wear "masks" to cover up the deep pain. We had to deal with the ugly truth about one another and the excessive anger, insecurities, mistrust, unforgiving spirits, betrayal, and sexual dysfunction hovered around. Junior would say "Ma, you take things too serious. You need to have fun and laugh sometime." Of course he was right, but I hadn't learned the secret to laughing through all the foolishness.

In spite of the difficult times, there were many opportunities to make good memories, and we took advantage of them. Yes, life was challenging but I refrained from saying "I'll be glad when this is over." I loved and enjoyed my children and appreciated our good times together realizing suffering is a part of life. This was my life.

## Preparation

I had slowly transformed from the quiet, reserved person I used to be to someone confident in the faith, doing things I hadn't done before. Not only was I teaching Sunday school, Junior Church, participating and orchestrating the teen events, but I took the initiative to start and teach a Wednesday night Teen Bible Study class. With Allison and Junior participating in the class, I was inspired to be a better listener and admit my own weaknesses and faults. Working with the teens gave me a better understanding of how family dynamics impacted their self-confidence and how they related to God.

Over the next ten year period, opportunities arose that challenged me to serve in capacities I had never dreamed of. At first I felt that I wasn't good enough for the things happening to me. Then I learned to speak positive to myself and expect great things.

## Oh No, Not Again!

I didn't realize how much I had grown spiritually and emotionally until I was put into situations where I performed public speaking, orchestrated social events, and became one of the cofounders of an annual women's conference that drew participants from a regional community. There had definitely been a change in my life and it was quite noticeable to my family and friends. My mother attended one of the conference sessions where I was the workshop speaker. After the session my mother walked up to me with amazement and proclaimed to everyone standing around "This can't be my daughter! Not Sharron who used to stay locked in her room all the time." It was a testimony of the great work God was doing in my life.

Soon I became a magnet that attracted hurting women. They shared a kindred spirit with me and were comfortable sharing their struggles and trials. Many were successful in their profession and carried themselves in a modest manner, but they had "masked" their internal hurts and pains. They needed someone to listen to and encourage them. I did so. I studied the Bible vigorously, read more Christian books on relationships, attended leadership conferences, and participated in numerous social events. I wanted to be fully equipped to help other hurting people. Life was challenging but I was looking at it from a positive perspective.

As a Christian I firmly believed in giving my tithes and offerings to the Lord. All that I had belonged to Him and He rewarded my faithfulness. I received numerous promotions and monetary awards on my job. For the first time I was thankful to Mom and Grandma for instilling a sense of excellence in me. I was determined and had the tenacity to excel in whatever I did. My supervisors saw my potential and I was selected for a 'career ladder' position where I was promoted twice within a two year period without having to further compete. This move advanced me into a midlevel management position. I was insecure about being in a management position over others from different walks of life and sometimes more educated, so I sought out a mentor to help build my knowledge base. My self-confidence grew as I claimed the promises in God's Word and learned to believe He would prepare me to do whatever He called me to do.

## Trouble Brewing

Over the ten year period of my metamorphosis, I learned to let go of Richard and stop trying to fix him and our marriage. After he recovered from his injuries and was able to get back into the workforce, he wanted to pursue his dream of being an entrepreneur. We didn't have a lot of money but utilized our resources to purchase a semi-tractor so Richard could start his own trucking business. He and I worked together to get the business started. He drove the rig and I did the administrative work.

Richard was great at what he did and I never doubted his success, although it was a couple of years before the business made a profit. He got the family involved and it was a great experience learning the industry. The boys and I loved riding with him during some of his trips. Not many people can say they achieved their dreams, but Richard could. He was happy doing what he'd always wanted to do and I was glad to be a part of it!

Unfortunately, with the success of the trucking business came Richard's pride, lies, and deceit. His desire for independence resurfaced. He claimed the business was his so he didn't need me or anyone else telling him what to do. As Richard spent less time at church, it wasn't long before he reverted to being a loner. Once again he put himself outside the area of accountability.

As Richard began staying away from home for longer periods at a time, lying about his whereabouts, and spending excessive amounts with no receipts to support it, I became suspicious of infidelity. However, I didn't approach him until I had solid evidence of his unfaithfulness. Even then he still denied it. Betrayal all over again! When would it end? I went through the process of forgiveness again, again, and again.

Though I forgave Richard, it was difficult to regain trust in him because he continued the same behavior but in a more discreet manner, or I should say he got better at being deceitful and "sneaky." Many times I wanted to bail out of our unhealthy marriage but I didn't believe that's what God wanted me to do at that point in my life. Tension ruled my home. The children were much older now and found it difficult to respect their father when they saw his actions and lack of remorse. We were actually relieved sometimes when Richard didn't come home.

## Oh No, Not Again!

Allison followed my advice and went away to college. Our mother-daughter relationship had strengthened and we communicated frequently. I wanted her to experience living in a dormitory and the full benefits of college life. After attending college for two years, Allison returned home to finish her requirements for nursing. She started dating and a year later we planned her wedding. My greatest fear for Allison and her fiancé was that they weren't aware of the ongoing complications resulting from the incest. Allison hadn't dealt with the forgiveness or trust issues and I knew that would carry over into her marriage relationship. I remembered how my life was impacted by childhood sexual abuse. It would take an emotionally strong and supportive husband to handle that type stress in a relationship.

It had been a long time since anyone talked about the incest, so I brought up the subject with Allison and her future husband. They were both confident they could handle any problems that might come up. But I knew better. I wondered if Allison was simply running from her problems. I quieted my fears and yielded to their decision. Richard and I supported Allison and gave her the beautiful church wedding she wanted. Thankfully Allison and I continued to spend time together. I longed to be the mother to her that she needed as she adjusted to adult life and marriage.

Junior desperately longed for his father's approval and attention. Richard, however, engaged more in his own interest than his son's. Junior harbored anger and resentment that affected his relationships with his siblings, girlfriends, and even me. He was a walking powder keg, easily ignited by the smallest things. He hadn't learned to control his anger but I was determined he wasn't going to overpower me. He was strong-willed and rebellious, but friendly and witty when he wanted to be. My greatest fear was that his uncontrolled anger would hurt someone. When he graduated from high school and showed no interest in going to college, I helped him fulfill his wishes of "getting out of this prison" by helping him leave the house.

Jeremy and Elizabeth were the only two children left at home. Jeremy silently carried his pain within. He wasn't interested in sports or hardly any other outside activities. His interest was in music, especially singing. Not only did he sing in our church and at his school, but others asked him to perform for their teen and youth functions. Richard didn't support Jeremy because he viewed his talents as "sissy stuff" and cruelly communicated that to him. However, whenever Jeremy was recognized for his accomplishments, Richard strutted about as the proud father. Jeremy had a promising career ahead of him but had a difficult time focusing on his goals.

Elizabeth did little to compete for her father's attention. Born during Richard's "period of contrition", Elizabeth was her daddy's little darling. Although Elizabeth was spoiled by three older siblings, she was a very confident and thoughtful child. As a young girl, she wrote notes and passed them out to people in the church when she perceived they needed encouragement. She was a happy child but could be very stubborn at times.

## What Are You Doing?

There was another child, Linda, who starved for Richard's attention and affection. Linda was Richard's daughter born outside our marriage a year before Jeremy was born. For all his faults, Richard was not a deadbeat dad and insisted on supporting and being a present factor in his child's life. In her earlier years, Linda often visited our home since I was uncomfortable with Richard going to her home to visit. I simply did not trust Richard. Over the years it became more difficult to treat Linda as part of the family when Richard shielded her from my discipline and showed favoritism toward her above the other children. Linda's visits in our home lessened although we continued to invite her to attend social events with us.

One night I had a dream about Richard and Linda. The dream came from nowhere but it seemed so real. Richard was molesting her. I wondered about the purpose of the dream. It was like God was revealing something to me. I lay there, hoping the dream was just a nightmare. There was no way he could do such a thing again, not after all the pain and trouble we had gone through already.

A couple of weeks later, I was informed by a close friend that Linda was with Richard on one of his long distance truck deliveries. This alarmed

## Oh No, Not Again!

me and I was suspicious. Richard hadn't mentioned anything about taking Linda with him, besides it was a weekday and she should have been in school. When I questioned Richard about it, he denied Linda had been with him. He hurled belittling comments at me, accusing me of making up stories and being suspicious because I wanted 'to find fault in him'. I learned that behavior was a clear indication that something was going on. If Richard wasn't already sexually abusing Linda, he was setting her up. I immediately went to Pastor Sander, who had befriended Richard, and asked if he could talk to him since I had no real proof of any sexual abuse. Pastor Sander listened but seemed to dismiss my concern. I was angry but powerless to do anything...I had nothing but my suspicion and a dream.

Approaching twenty five years of marriage I sat in my living room with the same feelings I had experienced twelve years prior when Allison revealed that her father was molesting her. Now I was concerned about another thirteen year old girl, not knowing what to do.

Linda lived with her sickly grandmother, a drug addicted mother, and two alcoholic uncles. Her home environment wasn't good and Richard had been her deliverer. At first I considered visiting them and warning them about Richard, but they all loved Richard and I was certain they would dismiss my suspicions. Then I realized if God gave me the dream, He would show me what to do. I would wait on Him.

In late August, a few months after the dream, the command where I worked released us early due to hurricane warnings. I went home to prepare the house and make sure we had adequate supplies in case the hurricane hit Norfolk. Turning into my street, I noticed Richard's car parked in front of the house. I wondered why he was home since he left earlier that day to take a trip out of town. I thought maybe his trip was cancelled due to the weather. I parked my car in the driveway and proceeded up to the house. As I unlocked the front door a funny feeling overwhelmed me. I looked down the hall and saw that my bedroom door was closed. I quietly walked down the hall and stood outside the door for a few seconds before gently turning the door knob. Richard was in my bed molesting Linda.

I stood there for a few seconds, motionless. They both looked up at me and Linda said "oops". I gently closed the door and walked away. Why I closed the door, I don't know. I walked to my car feeling numb. I got in the car and cried out, "Oh My God, You were preparing me for this. Oh Lord, not again!"

Although the weather was getting worse, I drove on Interstate 64 for several hours with tears flowing like a river and praying for God's guidance and comfort. "Lord, You know my heart's desire is to please you. Tell me how you want me to help Linda and I will." I cried for Linda. I cried for Richard because I knew what laid ahead for him. I cried for my children because they would go through this whole ordeal again! I cried for myself. Oh no, not again…not again!

The weather had gotten worse and the children didn't know my whereabouts. I knew they were home and I needed to be with them. When I walked in the house, Jeremy and Elizabeth noticed that I'd been crying but I didn't share with them what was going on. They were worried about me, so I reassured them of how much I loved them. We used the checklist to prepare for the hurricane and afterwards the children watched television in the den. I went into my bedroom, changed the bedding, and sat down. I needed to think. I didn't call my sisters or friends. I didn't even call Pastor Sander. I just wanted to be alone. Reclining on the bed, the children ran into my room asking about their father's whereabouts. The weather was getting worse but I assured them he was okay. I didn't know where Richard was and I didn't care. I didn't know if he was ever coming back again.

## You're Going Back

Late that night as heavy rains and strong winds raged outside, I heard the front door open. It was Richard. He headed straight for the den to watch television with the children. Of course the kids were excited to see him and know he was safe. Richard knew better than to come into the bedroom or to talk to me, so he wrote a note and sent it to me by Jeremy. In the letter Richard begged over and over again "I'm sorry, please don't report me. I don't want to go to jail again. I'll do what you want me to do. I'll get help. Please, please, please. Don't report me. I don't want to go back to jail." I didn't respond.

I continued reading my Bible so I could focus on the power of Christ. Meanwhile, Richard sent another letter saying some of the same things … he didn't want to go to jail and begging me not to report him. This time he added how much he loved me and thanked me for staying with him. I laid the note aside and told Jeremy not to bring me anything else from his dad. It was getting late so I sent the children to bed. I didn't want to face Richard. I didn't want to confront him. It was useless. Richard knew that I was going to report the sexual abuse. I certainly wasn't going to ignore the abuse and allow him to continue to molest Linda just because she wasn't my daughter. Although he sounded desperate and I felt sorry for him, nothing he said would stop me from doing what God put me in a position to do – report it.

The weather got worse throughout the night. Heavy rains poured down furiously, winds blew at high speeds tossing debris around, and trees swayed dangerously from side to side. Afraid of the noise outside Elizabeth and Jeremy climbed into my bed and curled up beside me. Bundled up together throughout the night, I watched my children sleep peaceably. There was so much turmoil outside yet they were resting because they were near me and felt protected.

I thought about my relationship with my Heavenly Father. There was so much turmoil going on all around me. I asked Him to speak peace to my situation and to calm the raging in my soul so I could rest. I visualized myself crawling up under Him and quoted Psalm 91:1 *"Whoever dwells in the shelter of the Most High will rest in the shadow of the Almighty."* Sometime during the early morning hours, I finally fell asleep.

When I woke up it was daylight and Richard was gone. I don't know when he left or where he went. I was ready to report the incest but due to the weather all government offices were closed. I had to wait another two days before I could report the incident to Child Protective Services.

The social worker thundered, "Why did you leave Linda in the bedroom with Richard after you witnessed the sexual abuse? What took you so long to report this?" Her first question was legitimate. I don't know why I left Linda there. The second question was a fluke, asked as if she didn't know we had severe damage from the hurricane and their office was closed. Sternly I replied, "Have you ever dealt with sexual abuse in your family?" She stopped moving papers around on her desk and looked directly at me. "No," she softly answered. I proceeded to inform her that words couldn't describe my pain. That's when she apologized for being so blunt.

As much as I wanted to hold back the tears, I was unsuccessful. Against my will, they trickled down my face. The CPS worker handed me a tissue and took my statement. I didn't know Linda's whereabouts or Richard's– he wasn't home.

The officials were able to locate Richard and arrest him. Afterwards he contacted me and called me a traitor. He used the same old blame game saying, "What kind of wife turns against her husband? Where's your loyalty?" I'd heard it all before and I wasn't going on any more "guilt trips." I finally realized that Richard was sick and I had to do what was right to protect society from him. I had to move on with my life – through the tears, broken heart and all.

## *Whispers on My Journey*

*On my journey through the furnace
I heard a whisper –
The Serenity Prayer
"God, grant me the serenity to accept the things
I cannot change; courage to change the things I can;
and wisdom to know the difference."
Reinhold Niebuhr*

*Most of my life I tried to control every situation and fix everything that was wrong. I tried to fix Richard in hopes of a better marriage. But I couldn't. However, I didn't believe in giving up on my family no matter how difficult it was to deal with matters. I never gave up on my children and I thought I was helping Richard by not giving up on him.*

*At times I felt powerlessness and unable to walk away from the unhealthy marriage relationship. I held onto my conviction that it was right to do right no matter what. I had no power to change Richard's life and no power to prevent the sexual abuse from happening to Linda. I had to accept the things I could not change.*

*But I had courage to change what I could. I reported it. Maybe in reporting the incest I spared Linda from becoming trapped in a lifestyle of pornography, promiscuous sexual activity, same sex attractions, drug addictions, alcoholism, isolation, bitterness, and a myriad of other vices that victims of child sexual abuse fall prey to in trying to deal with the shame of child sexual abuse. Allison had my support but I didn't know who would be there to help Linda.*

*I wasn't able to change my situation, nor get away from troubles, but I was able to change my attitude toward my circumstances. Life was messy and it wasn't within my power to alter the past. I just prayed, "LORD give me wisdom to know what I can change and what I can't, and the grace to live with the results." I believe in my weakness I learned to rely on God and His sufficiency.*

CHAPTER 12

# Pain, Pain, Go Away!

Sitting on the floor next to my bed, I realized many incidents happened in my bedroom. Ironically my bedroom was also my "secret closet" - the private place in my home where I enjoyed conversing with God. It's strange that the same bedroom where Richard chose to molest his daughters and where we struggled for intimacy was the same location I resorted to meet with God. I could even sleep there and not have visions or nightmares about the incest. I could go into the bedroom, close the door, and block everything out while I poured my heart out to the Lord. In those traumatic times I wished I had a father and mother to console me but I didn't. I knew my pain was not over yet.

### An Unbelievable Sentence
Richard was gone from the home for good. I was in the courtroom when the Judge pronounced Richard's sentence of twenty-five years! The Judge made him serve his suspended sentence from Allison's abuse since he was still on probation when he committed the offense against Linda. Twenty five years in the State Penitentiary. My chest felt tight like someone was squeezing me; I couldn't breathe. I went to my car and released the flood of tears I had desperately held back. "Twenty five years"…I kept repeating it. The courts had sent a clear message that sexual abuse would not be tolerated. Although I felt terrible that Richard was incarcerated, I was relieved that justice was served and that he wouldn't hurt another child. At the same time, I thought about my children and how they would react to growing up without their father.

Twenty five years was the same number of years Richard and I were married when he molested Linda…not that it had any significance. It was interesting that the severity of his sentence corresponded to the years of our troubled marriage. Putting my feelings aside, I prepared to break the news to Jeremy and Elizabeth, who had waited almost ten months to hear the sentencing. When I told them the news, they both cried uncontrollably. Jeremy was thirteen and had never received the affection and love from his father that he craved; nevertheless, he loved him and grieved that his father would be in prison until he was an adult. Before the abuse to Linda, Elizabeth had never been away from her father for more than a week at a time, so twenty-five years seemed forever for my eight year old.

Allison and Junior were young adults living away from home, but their painful memories resurfaced. They were filled with anger that their siblings would suffer the shame and embarrassment they had experienced. I was faced with the challenges of being a single parent again and trying to help my children cope with the situation.

## Need for Encouragement

My church family meant so much to me and having spent ten years serving in ministries with them, I expected lots of support and encouragement after Richard was arrested. Unfortunately, the place I loved to minister was now a place where I sensed a lack of belonging. Sexual abuse wasn't something talked about in our church. No one knew how to minister to me and my children's sufferings in the aftermath of it. No one acknowledged that Richard was incarcerated or that my children were distraught. Maybe it was impossible for them to know the pain we felt, especially if they had not experienced it and the subject was not discussed.

I was strong in my faith and maybe did not show any signs of distress. I was guilty of not communicating with others how this ordeal was affecting us. I discussed the issue with Pastor Sander but he didn't seem to understand how much I needed emotional support because I proved to be joyous in the midst of many trials I encountered before.

Pain, Pain, Go Away!

I tried to continue teaching the teen Bible study but eventually stepped down from the leadership position. I was discouraged and my focus shifted from ministering to others with needs to concerns about what people were not doing for my family. As I went through my grief process I was made aware of how others probably felt when they came to church and went through the expected "motions" but felt alone when they left the place of worship. Armed with that revelation, I refused to continue in my defeated mental state. I sought a healing ministry where I could grieve without feeling condemned and learn to serve others through my brokenness.

My children and I found a church where I could minister and help others while being ministered to. Our new pastor often referred to his church as a "spiritual hospital" because of the work God called him to do in ministering to hurting people. It was the right place for us to be at that time in our lives. Pastor Gray and his wife were not strangers to us. We attended our previous church together. They knew Richard and had tried to minister to him before he was incarcerated the second time.

As members we experienced God's favor and overwhelming blessings. I didn't serve in any ministry at church until we were there for three to four months. Then Pastor Gray said "It's time for you to start and teach a women's Sunday school class." I strived to help others to grow in their faith in the midst of their trials. Later, I was asked to direct the women's ministry. My healing came as I applied biblical principles to my life and spent time serving others.

## Sexual Identity Crisis

I couldn't give but so much time to ministry at church because I still had a special area of home ministry that required my time. I regularly took Jeremy and Elizabeth to visit their father in the penitentiary. As long as they wanted to see him, I made it possible. I believed in protecting my children but I didn't believe it was my "right" to deny them a relationship with their father.

The Virginia Department of Corrections constantly moved Richard from one prison to another. Some of the places were a several hours away from home, but we still managed to visit Richard a couple times a month.

After three years of visiting his father in prison, Jeremy decided he was tired of spending time with a father who expressed minimal interest in things that were important to him. Richard hadn't changed - no remorse nor repentance. Jeremy was sixteen and struggling with his sexual identity. He couldn't talk to his father and wouldn't talk to me about it. Then Jeremy decided to openly announce he was homosexual. I didn't know how to handle his choice of lifestyle; it went against everything I believed. Jeremy and I constantly engaged in heated theological debates about it. We were divided on this issue and it brought tension between us. He professed to be a Christian but was determined to live the lifestyle he wanted, no matter how I felt or what I said. I didn't know what to do or where to turn for help.

Listening to my favorite radio station as I was driving home from work one day, I heard an author being interviewed about her book. She shared that when her son confessed he was homosexual, she and her husband pushed him out of their lives and had no dealings with their son for ten years. The author was brokenhearted as she told of receiving a phone call from a young man on the verge of suicide. She found out the young man was homosexual and had been ostracized by his family. He was lonely, depressed, and hadn't known a mother's love in a long time. The author was reminded of the son she rejected. She missed him and wondered if he felt the same way this young man felt. She had repented for the decision she made.

As I listened intently to the author, I wept. That's when I decided that Jeremy would always be a part of my life. Setting boundaries was arduous because I couldn't compromise my beliefs neither could I deny him my love. Trying to support Jeremy's dreams and ambitions without encouraging his lifestyle was almost impossible and generated much friction between the two of us. If there weren't arguments about sexual integrity

## Pain, Pain, Go Away!

on the internet, there were arguments about him respecting the rules in my house. Jeremy questioned everything he had been taught.

After graduating from high school, Jeremy refused to go to college. I tried to help him get established on his own, but he had other ideas and just wanted to hang out with his friends all hours of the night.

Finally, with a broken heart, I put Jeremy out of my house so he could establish his own independence. It was a tough decision and I cried so much as I worried about his safety. My house became a revolving door to Jeremy because when things didn't go as he planned, he would come back home. After a couple years, I finally stopped rescuing Jeremy, as I realized he was old enough to make decisions and had the freedom to live his life the way he chose. He had to live with the consequences of his actions. Reluctantly, I had to cut the "apron string"…he wasn't my little boy anymore; he was a grown man. I had to respect his choices and exercise "tough love."

I couldn't help but wonder how the incest and family dysfunction influenced Jeremy's actions and shaped his beliefs. Mentally I fought against the notion there was a curse of sexual dysfunction on our family. It took a long time to see how generational attitudes had been passed on and that even as a Christian, I cultivated an environment that allowed the dysfunction to continue. I was determined to break the mold. I tried to do what was right, but it seemed that more trials and hardships came into our family.

### Teen Pregnancy

After Jeremy left home, it was just Elizabeth and I. She continued to visit her father in prison a few more years then concluded Richard had very little concern about the things that were of interest to her. A short time later, she let me know she and Richard had so little to talk about that she no longer wanted to visit. Elizabeth yearned for her father's attention but not getting it, she looked elsewhere. Young, attractive, and popular, Elizabeth became interested in boys and enjoyed their attention, even when it was inappropriate.

Elizabeth and I were still going to church and spending time together. Although we talked about most things, we couldn't come to agreement about her unhealthy interest in boys or her unsuitable dress attire. During a period when I worked mandatory overtime, Elizabeth took advantage of the opportunity to sneak out the house and hang with friends that I wouldn't approved of. I noticed a greater change in her. Elizabeth stopped talking about her feelings and began to act rebellious toward me. She was acting totally out of character and it got my attention. On one occasion I knocked on her forehead and said "Will the real Elizabeth please come out?" She snickered and accused me of being silly.

At fifteen years old, I hadn't given Elizabeth permission to date but that didn't stop her from secretly having a boyfriend. I suspected it and tried on several occasions to talk to Elizabeth about it. She denied it. I even tried to talk about sex and questioned Elizabeth about being sexually active. Of course she denied it. One night I couldn't sleep. The possibility of Elizabeth being pregnant caused me to toss and turn most of the night. I tried to dismiss the thoughts but I couldn't. I had that feeling again that God was revealing something to me. Later that week Allison was at the house. Watching Elizabeth as she left the room, she said "Momma is she pregnant?" Allison, a registered nurse was very observant and suspected pregnancy because of the way Elizabeth carried herself. Allison's comment and my sleepless night were reason enough for me to purchase a home pregnancy kit. When I got home, I sent Elizabeth in the bathroom. When she brought the stick to me I exclaimed "O my Lord! Elizabeth is only fifteen and she's pregnant!" My heart was so heavy. I knew the life ahead for my daughter ...what it was like being a teen parent.

## No Perfect Children

No matter how much I loved my children and wanted the best for them, they made their own decisions. It seemed like all our problems revolved around unhealthy sexual activity. Feeling a little depressed one morning and apathetic toward life, I dragged around the house as I slowly prepared for work. "They better be glad that I show up for work today," I mused.

Leaving the house a little later than usual, I turned on my favorite radio station and a program caught my attention. The speaker was saying, "I try to do so much for my children." She took her responsibility seriously. She went on to articulate all the things she did to raise good children. Then she said "While others are bragging on their children's accomplishments, I feel like a failure because my children haven't achieved all the accolades of others. Mine weren't even trying. God, I've failed at being a mother!" She had my undivided attention because I was feeling the same way. My children had made some unwise decisions and I felt like I should have been a better mother.

The speaker continued "God asked me a profound question. Am I a good Parent?"

She quickly replied "Yes Lord" and began to tell God how great He is. "You're loving, just, patient, kind, and holy. You're a good listener, protector, provider, role model, always providing the best for your children, You administer discipline in a loving way and extend mercy and grace whenever needed. Yes, Lord You're awesome and the perfect parent!"

Then God responded "Then what's wrong with My children?"

I burst out laughing. I laughed so hard I was teary eyed. I hadn't laughed like that in a long time. I said out loud "God you are the perfect parent...and yet You have some messed up children - and I happen to be one of them."

That was just the message I needed to hear that morning. I needed reassurance that my children's problems weren't an indication that I wasn't a good mother. I did the best I knew how and now I had to focus on helping Elizabeth as she embarked on motherhood.

When I talked to Elizabeth, I wanted to know what she wanted to do about the pregnancy. I said "You have three options and each has consequences. You need to decide which is best for you. You can terminate the pregnancy, give the child up for adoption, or raise your own baby." I continued with "adoption isn't bad. There're a lot of couples wanting a newborn baby. Your baby would be placed in a wonderful home with loving parents." I glossed over the option of abortion in hopes she wouldn't consider it because of my beliefs against it. I sat quietly giving her a few minutes to think. Then she responded "Momma I could never kill my child. And I can't live my life knowing I have a child out there that will never know me or understand why I didn't want him. I want to raise my own baby." It was the decision I hoped for and I was pleased that it was her decision. As her mother, I promised to help her raise her child.

I knew the challenges Elizabeth would face mothering a child while she was so immature herself. She had a lot of growing up to do and maternal responsibilities would come quickly. In spite of the pregnancy and obstacles stacked against her, Elizabeth was determined to graduate from high school. Like me, she had tenacity and determination. She would be a great mother and I would be available to help her.

### *Whispers on My Journey*

***On my journey through the furnace***
***I heard a whisper –***
***"Many are the afflictions of the righteous,***
***but the Lord delivers him out of them all."***
***Psalm 34:19***

*Excruciating pain mixed with exuberant faith was the best description of my life. I learned to have joy in the midst of my sorrows. I stopped wishing each day would quickly pass and I quit saying "I'll be glad when this is over" because if it wasn't one thing it was something else.*

*I pondered over the goodness of the Lord that He didn't abandon me nor was He ashamed of me because I made foolish decisions. Just like He extended mercy toward me, I wanted to show that same love and compassion to my children as they rebelled against the foundational things I taught them. My heart was so heavy, my tears so many, and my prayers so frequent on their behalf. I was helpless in rescuing them or solving their problems. They had to learn to trust the Lord to do that.*

*I held onto my greatest weapon - praise. In the midst of my afflictions when the pain was so intense it was almost unbearable, I sang praises to the Lord for being the wonderful God that He is and thanked Him for all the hardships as well as the wonderful moments in life.*

*This was my life and I wouldn't exchange it with anyone else. I thought of a saying I heard: "When life deals you a lemon, make lemonade."*

*I understood the concept and stopped complaining and belittling myself. I was a good parent and I was committed to my children. I gave of myself regardless of their situation.*

*There was something good in everything. Through my affliction I learned to love the Lord more and more. Through affliction I developed character. Through affliction I cultivated empathy for others. I knew all the trials I experienced weren't only for me, but to help someone else as well.*

CHAPTER 13

# For A Purpose

Life had its challenges, but the victories over the hurts and pains of the past helped me make it through my next challenge. I reflected over my life and my transformation. It was encouraging seeing the change in my life. Despite all my trials, afflictions, and sufferings, I had a purpose in life. I wasn't just surviving from one day to the next. I was beginning to live life to its fullest.

## Illness for a Purpose

I did my best to help Elizabeth enjoy her pregnancy, but she wasn't my only challenge. When Elizabeth was in her seventh month of pregnancy, I discovered a mass during one of my regular breast examinations. Knowing many women die from breast cancer I got immediate medical attention. After being examined by my breast specialist I was scheduled for a mammogram and later a biopsy. The diagnosis was breast cancer.

My specialist, the very best in the Tidewater area, took the time to meet with my family members and educated us about cancer and available treatments. My family, friends, and church members continued to join me in prayer for healing. Although I wasn't healed immediately as I preferred, I had the assurance that God would heal me even if it was through surgery and treatments. At this point in my life I was always looking for God to do something great. I believed "extreme persecution…extreme blessings."

The morning of my surgery I anticipated something great would happen. My children, sisters, mother, and Pastor Gray came to the hospital to be with me and give me moral support. After being prepped for surgery, my pastor came into the pre-op area and asked if he could have a word of prayer with me before they took me to surgery. My surgeon was about to excuse herself so we could have some privacy when Pastor Gray invited her to stay and join us. I could tell she was totally surprised but she joined with us as my pastor not only prayed for me but for her as well. At the conclusion of the prayer, my surgeon expressed how thankful she was that someone thought enough of her to pray that God would give her wisdom, guide her hands, and bless her to be His instrument in the healing process. This surgery was more than just removing the mass from my breast, but it was about ministering to others in the process.

A few days later I received the lab results from the tissue and lymph nodes that were removed. It showed a very slight possibility of metastases. I was scheduled for more visits with my oncologist and had to undergo various bone scans, x-rays, blood tests, and examinations. Finally, I received radiation treatments for several weeks.

## Healed for a Purpose

Before my radiation treatments began, Elizabeth gave birth to a beautiful son, Deon. It was no accident that his birth was couched between my surgery and my treatments. My illness wasn't about death but the beauty of life. It was wonderful to hold that innocent newborn during my physical healing process. There were days when I finished my radiation treatments and a half day at work, that I was refreshed by holding Deon in my arms and singing some of my favorite songs, one of which was "Jesus Loves Me."

There were so many blessings God sent my way while I was undergoing the medical treatment. I had the support of all my children, my sisters, my friends, and my coworkers as well. It was evident that during my trials and sufferings I had learned the value of relationships. It was my answer to prayer that trials brought us closer together. We could count on the support of each other.

Not only did I recuperate physically, but I was emotionally healthy as well. I believed holistic healing had finally taken place. I was free from the burden of incest, sexual abuse, same sex addictions and the guilt as if I had caused them. I was enjoying life. I no longer felt the need to hang on to an unhealthy marriage that showed no signs of reconciliation. Ten years had passed since Richard's incarceration and although I continued to visit him occasionally after Jeremy and Elizabeth stopped, I still saw no signs of remorse or him taking ownership of his problem with incest, so our thirty-five year marriage ended.

That same year Elizabeth graduated from high school and I received my Master's Degree. To celebrate these major achievements, - Allison, her daughter Cherie, Elizabeth, and I took our first cruise and sailed off to the Bahamas. I wanted to see the world and all the beauty God created. Being within the five year window for retirement I also wanted to fulfill my dream of working overseas. I had only been overseas once and that was five years prior when Elizabeth and I went on a missionary trip to Haiti. I knew then that I wanted to experience living in another culture. For the first time in my life, there was nothing to hold me back from achieving my dreams.

After submitting job applications and much prayer, I received a phone interview for a position at a military base in Japan. I did my research and waited for confirmation from the Lord to proceed. My answer came the following Sunday during the morning worship service. I can't remember what the pastor preached but after church I got my best friend Brenda situated in the car and put her wheelchair in the trunk, as usual. As I took my place in the driver's seat. I looked at Brenda without saying a word. She stared back at me and said "you're going to Japan." "Yes!" I smiled.

While waiting several months for my medical and legal paperwork to process, I was scheduled to attend a conference in Leesburg, Virginia in preparation for my new position in Yokosuka, Japan. It was there that I met Charles Dansby who had worked four years in a similar position at the same command where I was assigned to work. He supplied information

## For A Purpose

and educated me on the unique Japanese workforce I would supervise, the community events, and the Christian ministries he participated in. Charles was very helpful, friendly, and single.

One of my best friends, Ro, was working in Bahrain and had attended the conference also. As girlfriends talk, she brought it to my attention that Charles seemed to be very interested in me. I informed her that he may be a potential friend, nothing more and nothing less. I wasn't interested in a dating relationship.

## Go for a Purpose

After celebrating Christmas, I packed my suitcases and left my family and friends and boarded the plane for my 13 ½ hour flight to Japan. Arriving at Narita Airport on New Year's Eve was a totally new experience. Clearing Customs and not being able to read the congee on the walls around the airport made me uncomfortable for a moment. Then I noticed Charles and a female friend from the Singles Ministry at Yokosuka Naval Base waiting to escort me to my destination.

Life was really interesting in Japan. Charles and I became best friends as we worked and explored Japan together. Then Elizabeth came over and later Deon joined us. Then Jeremy came over for a while. They got to know Charles and soon loved him. He was such a gentleman. I admired his dedication to the Lord and faithfulness in ministry and service. The men held him in high regard. Americans and Japanese spoke highly of him. I was glad to be his friend. It felt good to laugh and have fun. It felt good to be respected and admired. Charles was good for me and good to me.

I don't know when the friendship escalated to something more serious, but it felt so good to be loved. For months we denied that we were in love until Elizabeth and several other friends started making comments about our "close" friendship.

Faced with a dilemma of what I should do about our friendship, I did the only thing I knew how to do and that was to pray for guidance and seek counsel from my godly friends. I sent an email to my friend Ro who was working in Bahrain. We had been friends for over twenty years and were always there to support one another through our hardships, trials, and drama with jobs, husbands and children. When I told her my friendship with Charles was getting serious, I expected a response similar to "Girl, get a hold of yourself and tell Charles to back off…you don't need that drama…run girl run!" Instead she responded with something totally unexpected saying "Sharron, you've been hurt so much. I know you want to be careful and only want God's best for your life. Don't be afraid to let God bless you." I read her comments over and over again and couldn't believe her words…so we talked.

Months later Charles proposed to me. He had already prayed about marriage and was convinced I would be his wife the first day he met me in Leesburg. I didn't have that assurance. I couldn't trust my heart because it had deceived me before. For the first time in my thirty years of walking with the Lord, I prayed and asked God to give me a "sign" to validate that I should marry Charles. I also asked Pastor Gray to pray about the marriage because if God wanted us to marry, he would be the one to officiate the ceremony. God gave me a "sign."

Charles and I flew from Japan to my home church in Portsmouth, Virginia for a wedding our family coordinated. It was an awesome, humbling experience to join in holy matrimony with Charles and to have family and friends in Virginia, and friends who came from Japan to participate in our wedding. After the glorious ceremony and a fantastic honeymoon, we returned to Japan and lived there another three years. The next year, we were pleased to enjoy the company of Allison and my granddaughter Cherie and exposed them to the Japanese culture.

## Called for a Purpose

Charles and I believed the Lord had a mandate on us and would use us to help others in bondage and enslaved to addictive behaviors. Having completed our overseas assignment, we left Japan for jobs in Washington, D.C. I was amazed to be promoted again and reached the height of my career.

# For A Purpose

We joined First Baptist Church of Glenarden where we are serving others and supporting the church's mission of "developing dynamic disciples." God is giving me and Charles opportunities to minister and help those who are hurting and in especially those in bondage due to sexual sins. My prayer is that the details of my life may be used to encourage others as they travel on their journey to seek healing, deliverance and wholeness. I continue to pray for transformation and restoration that will impact generations to come.

By the power of God I love my mother and have become the mother I want to be. I enjoy the company of my children and ten grandchildren. I love the relationship I have with my sisters, nieces, and nephews. I have more true friends than I ever dreamed possible. I've learned to be transparent thankful for the miraculous work the Lord has done in my life. I live each day with great anticipation of what He will do next. The journey was rough, but it was certainly worth it.

## *Whispers on My Journey*

*On my journey through the furnace
I heard a whisper –
"For I know the thoughts that I think toward you,
says the LORD, thoughts of peace and not of evil,
to give you a future and a hope."
Jeremiah 29:11*

*I really didn't understand the reason behind all the trials and pain in my life but I wanted to have Job's attitude. When God gave Satan permission to test Job, Job lost his children, his wealth, and his health. The Bible said "Job arose, tore his robe, and shaved his head; and he fell to the ground and worshiped and he said 'Naked I came from my mother's womb, and naked shall I return there. The LORD gave, and the LORD has taken away; Blessed be the name of the LORD." Job 1:20-21. After Job suffered and prayed for his friends that wrongfully accused him of secret sin, God blessed Job with twice as much as he had before.*

*Not claiming to be Job or even daring to compare my sufferings with his, I too realized everything I possessed came from God and it was His to take away. When I embraced that truth and the fact that He loved me unconditionally, then I surrendered and said, "Lord, have your way." It was His plan for me to suffer and then bless me with more than I ever could imagine. Only the Lord of the universe could take my tragedies and turn them into blessings and use me to bless others. To God be the glory!*

CHAPTER 14

# Now That I Know

Of all the difficult things I have encountered, writing this book was high on the list. Nevertheless, I wrote with a passion and desire to help others understand the trauma of child sexual abuse and its devastating effects. I have been transparent in sharing my experiences and how sexual abuse affected me in the long term. It must be noted that not only does the primary survivor suffer, but also the secondary survivors as well - the family and loved ones. Even the community at large suffers from this tragic epidemic.

"Stranger danger" is real, especially with the rise of human trafficking. There is a great necessity to protect children from perpetrators who "groom" their victims from families that trust them. Having exposed the secrets concerning our family I wanted to reflect on some lessons learned while on my journey through the furnace.

The axiom, "ignorance is bliss," implies that a lack of knowledge results in happiness, is *totally* not true. It may *feel* comfortable in not knowing certain things because knowledge may require action. It is also said that "hindsight is 20/20 vision." Meaning we usually see the effect of things more clearly after they happen. Life is all about making decisions. If I could go back and make different decisions, I would. However, that is not an option. Therefore, I want to share a few things that I learned in order to educate others and possibly prevent another child from the traumatic experience and long term effects of child sexual abuse.

## Grooming

Growing up, I didn't have close friends. Neither did my siblings. The isolation made us more vulnerable to keeping secrets. I met Richard when I was 13; he was eight years my senior. He was interested in me and quickly became my best friend. Richard showered me with so much attention that I didn't mind keeping our secrets. He had brought so much happiness into my broken world. I was in love!

However, in a few short years, I experienced betrayal that words could never describe. Having grown up in a home void of affection, as a married woman I tolerated Richard's verbal and emotional abuse because I was so insecure and starved for love and acceptance. There were serious troubles in our marriage before the trauma with Allison occurred but sexual abuse never entered my mind whenever I left her and my other children alone with their father. After all, we were a family and he was their biological father! What I did not know about the nature of child sexual abuse came to haunt me. I didn't know anything about the grooming process where perpetrators lure or entrap a child into becoming a victim.

There was one incident, however, that made me uncomfortable. I should have been suspicious of Richard's interaction with Allison on that particular day. Richard had driven up in the driveway. Allison looked out the window and when she saw him, she quickly ran away from the window. When Richard entered the house, he walked straight o Allison and gave her a set of earrings. They were very pretty. I thought that was kind of strange since it wasn't Allison's birthday or any other special occasion. Richard wasn't one to shower us with affection or gifts, neither did he and Allison have a close father-daughter relationship, but I reasoned within myself that he was only trying to be nice. Allison took the earrings without expressing any type of gratitude and went directly to her bedroom.

Later, I saw the earrings unpackaged laying on Allison's dresser. I asked her why her father had given her the earrings and she muttered "I don't know." Of course she didn't know "why" he gave her the earrings. I had asked the wrong question. At that time I was unaware of the signs of sexual abuse. I could have protected Allison had I known them and pursued to find out more. I have learned that there are levels of progression, called "grooming" that precedes the molestation.

First, perpetrators befriend their victims and make them feel special in order to gain their trust. Then the perpetrator begins to engage in inappropriate behavior leading up to the molestation and assault. The child then is encouraged to keep secrets or in some cases, the perpetrators may threaten to hurt someone the child loves.

I often think about how Allison and Linda who were close to the age of 13 when Richard molested them (the same age I was when he befriended me). Was there a pattern? I do suspect that perpetrators have their age and gender preferences.

## Missing the Signs

Unlike physical abuse, there may be little physical evidence that a child is being sexually abused. However, I did notice changes in Allison's behavior. She was eating more junk foods, gaining weight, lacked interest in doing anything or participating in activities she had enjoyed in the past. She was frequently depressed and began to isolate herself even from other family members.

Allison had plenty of reasons to act the way she did. I knew she was a lot like me…an introvert who didn't like anyone pushing her outside her comfort zone. She gave her best but felt so defeated when she didn't get the desired outcome, like not being selected as a cheer leader or not winning piano recital competitions. She just wasn't very competitive. Being a preteen wasn't easy – at least that was the explanation I accepted.

I took pride in the fact that Allison was my compliant child. She was always eager to please and avoided confrontation whenever possible. Her frequent stomach aches I excused as female issues because I suffered with them too. Her withdrawal, poor self-esteem and lack of friends were not abnormal to me because that is how I grew up as a child. Also, our home was not conducive to having friends around. We seldom invited anyone to come over because we were afraid of how Richard would act – that he would embarrass us or them.

I couldn't clearly understand Allison's cry for help because I was experiencing some of the same behaviors. Little did I know that I was still struggling with long term effects of my own childhood sexual abuse. Since I had never disclosed the sexual abuse that happened to me, or recieved any help to deal with it, I was unable to recognize the signs that it was happening to Allison.

## Survivors

Allison, Roberta, Precious, Kay, Linda, and I were all primary survivors. I shared each of our experiences with sexual abuse to show the similarities of its traumatic impact. In addition to us, there were some other survivors- our children and close relatives. They are the secondary survivors. When I reported Allison's sexual abuse, I didn't know how Junior, Jeremy, and Elizabeth would respond. I shared their stories and the impact the abuse had on their lives and their decision making process because many of the same struggles primary survivors experienced are also experienced by the secondary survivors. In our home not only did Allison suffer but Junior, Jeremy and Elizabeth also struggled with insecurity, poor self-esteem, lack of self-worth, depression and other symptoms…Junior's rebellious behavior, Jeremy's struggle with sexual identity, and Elizabeth's inappropriate conduct in her search for a father's love.

I don't believe we can break the chains of the sexual abuse if we don't disclose it. Secrets allowed it to happen in the first place. Maybe some people don't report the sexual abuse in order to avoid the emotional or financial pain that usually accompanies the disclosure. Many children don't disclose the sexual abuse because of fear: fear of not being believed, fear of getting someone in trouble, fear of rejection, fear of being punished - just to name a few. Sometimes that same fear is present when adult survivors first disclose their abuse. People may wonder why it took so long to disclose the abuse or why do it now (sometimes 20 years or more later). Often there's the unfounded guilt of thinking the sexual abuse is something they should have gotten over by now.

Once I knew about Allison's abuse, it required action. I could not be silent or turn a blind eye to what had happened. I knew I had to report the abuse in order for it to stop, but I didn't know then how deeply the emotional pain caused by that abuse would affect me and my children. There was no way of avoiding the pain. Even so, I preferred to suffer for doing the right thing because I knew some good would result from it.

## Long term effects

I had no idea that being sexually abused as a child had long term effects which carried into adulthood. I thought the sexual abuse that happened to me was something that just happened and that I should try to forget about it. I was able to bury the memories for a while and subconsciously I developed unhealthy coping skills. It was a traumatic experience to be violated by someone I trusted, especially at such a young age of development. I believe the sexual abuse contributed to my poor self-esteem, insecurities, lack of self-worth, depression, suicidal thoughts, loss of trust, isolation, guilt, shame, poor decision making, and uncomfortable feelings toward intimacy and sexual activity. I didn't like my body and was careful not to expose it any more than necessary, even to the point of sleeping under the covers regardless of the temperature. When I covered up, I felt safe. I even carried that into marriage.

The pain and trauma caused by child sexual abuse isn't erased by time. No survivor should have to walk the path of disclosure and recovery alone, but change has to happen within. My life began to change for the better the night I knelt beside my bed and invited Jesus to come in to my life. Over the next few weeks, I found a great church and pastor that preached from the Bible. Through their friendships and the application of biblical principles, God began the process of healing me from the trauma of the child sexual abuse I had experienced. The emotional healing was painful at times, just like any physical healing. Periodically I still tried to take control because I wanted to be perfect (although taking control in the past had never worked out). I had to learn to be vulnerable and face the truth about myself, my fears, and my limitations. I spent more time in the scriptures and began to memorize and apply them in my life. Healing took place as I made it a priority to read the bible, pray to God with a sincere and open heart, and deal with my feelings rather than ignore them.

Pastoral counseling further helped me take off the mask. It was only then that I began to establish friendships with people going in the direction that I desperately wanted to go. I realized I could not live this life alone. Not only did I need the help of others, I need their love and acceptance. I'm so thankful for those who gave it to me.

## Wife of a Perpetrator

It was exactly eight years from the time I received Jesus into my life that I found out Allison was being molested. I had enough support and inner strength by then to enable me to report it. This began a whole series of legal, financial, and emotional challenges. Once again I tried to smooth the way and handle all the major challenges.

I remember the words of a man who attended Parents United with Richard and I, "you do everything for Richard and he hates you for it" he surmised. I wanted a family so badly that I did everything I could to hold us together. At that time I even wanted to keep Richard from suffering the consequences of his actions or at least minimize them. That included putting up with Richard's continual infidelity and verbal abuse. A friend of mine said "you can choose your sin, but you can't choose the consequences." Throughout my journey, I learned that each person has to take responsibility for his or her own actions.

There weren't many marriages in our families. At sixteen when I married Richard I wanted to beat the odds. I wanted our marriage to work so I tolerated Richard's verbal abuse, infidelity, controlling behavior, and uncontrollable anger. I didn't want to give up the dream of one day having the family I always longed for. Even after his continual infidelity, the sexual abuse, and the pain of betrayal, I still hoped Richard and I could work out our marriage. However, I didn't know the depth of both of our emotional issues.

After I reported the sexual abuse on Allison, Richard and I began court-ordered counseling. I had to discuss the details of the sexual abuse that I had experienced as a child. Later during the court preparation, I found out that Richard too was a victim. I couldn't understand how someone who experienced such pain could inflict it upon someone else. I couldn't help but feel sorry for Richard but that didn't erase the pain. Neither of us had dealt with our childhood sexual abuse.

I enjoyed reading self-help books. Two of the subjects I read a lot about were being codependent and an enabler. I realized that unknowingly I had made it easier for Richard to continue his destructive behavior and had supported his irresponsibility. These were issues I had to deal with in order to engage in any healthy relationship. I have often regretted allowing Richard to come back home and be around Allison. If I could reverse that decision, I would.

## Support Systems

Child sexual abuse is a taboo subject. We know that it happens, but we don't want to talk about it. Even in church many have a lack of understanding or awareness of child sexual abuse. Many are misinformed of the long term effects on survivors. It's hard to comprehend how someone you see every week in church is capable of molesting a child, especially their own. Even coaches, daycare providers, teachers, ministers, or anyone other adult dedicated to helping children might actually befriend a child for the sake of victimizing them.

I encountered well-meaning professionals who didn't understand the trauma associated with child sexual abuse. My family had been shattered! Richard couldn't return home without the approval of the "system." In less than two years after the abuse he was approved to return home with no accountability –just a suspended sentence hanging over his head. I didn't realize then that it was too soon for Richard to return home. I didn't realize the need of a support system for Allison in addition to me and her aunts.

Counseling had helped me but I only attended for a short period of time. I wish I had continued longer. After disclosing Allison's abuse I realized I had so many issues to deal with. I felt that a support group would help to deal with them. Parents United was the one support group I attended but I found very little support there, primarily because the perpetrators were present and so much attention was given to dealing with their issues. I also belonged to two different churches, at separate times, during the times I reported the incest that had been forced on both Allison and Linda. At neither time was the issue of molestation or incest discussed nor was there a support group within either church family. People appeared more comfortable hiding the issue or ignoring it.

I am so grateful that I had a few people who did support me and Allison - my sisters, brother and sister in laws, close friends, Mrs. Betty who took Allison shopping, and the man who took Jeremy bowling. I truly appreciate their random acts of kindness. Survivors truly need a support system where they can be transparent and honest without the fear of judgment.

Currently I belong to a church where there is a ministry for survivors of child sexual abuse and I facilitate one of the groups. It has made a difference in the lives of women who are dealing with the long term effects of being abused some as long as 10-25 years ago. Some are just now disclosing what happened to them, the circumstances surrounding the abuse, how they suffered from not being believed or blamed for the abuse, and the impact the sexual abuse had on their emotional stability and relationships.

## Forgiveness

I often wondered when the pain would go away: the betrayal of trust, the guilt, the shame, the emotional pain, the excessive anger and the negative thinking. It began to happen when I learned to have a forgiving spirit. Some people asked me how I could forgive Richard. I didn't want to forgive him or anyone else that hurt me because I wanted my abusers to suffer as much as I had and I didn't want to minimize the abuse. But that's not how it worked. I was the prisoner. They hurt me….then I began to hurt myself over and over again by holding grudges and anger against them. Then I learned about biblical forgiveness. As stated previously in Chapter 9, I didn't want to forgive but I loved God so much that I knew I had to follow His leading. I knew that obedience would be worth it.

At first the idea of forgiveness seemed impossible. I learned from experience that it was a way of life and not a one-time event. When I forgave Richard, I wasn't excusing him of the abuse neither was I cancelling out the fact that he should be held accountable for his actions through the judicial system. I had to care about him and learn to see him as God saw him. I had to relinquish the mindset to seek revenge as I considered what Christ did on the cross for me and the kindness He showed to me. Christ Himself experienced abuse and yet He chose to forgive.

I knew all this in my head but it was only by growing into an intimate relationship with Jesus Christ was I able to forgive. I had to learn to serve Richard before I could truly realize and appreciate the depth and impact of real forgiveness. Dan Allender, - author, president, and professor of counseling at Mars Hill Graduate School in Seattle, WA stated it so well:

*"The gift of doing good to an abuser is a postponement of the legitimate desire for revenge and justice for the sake of seeing the abuser restored to God and eventually to the one he abused. Forgiveness is letting go of hatred and bitterness so that the passion of the gospel and boldness of love can fill our hearts."*

## Restoration

The reality is that forgiveness is not reconciliation. When Richard returned home from jail I thought our relationship would be reconciled. We both had been through so much and our children needed us. However, reconciliation requires repentance. That ingredient was absent as Richard constantly reminded me that nothing was wrong with him and that I was the reason he was the way he was. Early in our marriage I actually believed that lie, but I finally learned that we must all take responsibility for our own actions. I knew that I must do right even if Richard didn't. I had to give an account to God for myself.

I stayed in the marriage with Richard for 35 years. I learned the valuable lesson of putting God first and loving others. People who know me realize without a doubt that I love the Lord with all my heart. That's because He has truly been with me through the furnace. My life has been a difficult journey, but God has been there with me all the way. Every area of my life had to be restored to the beauty God intended. There are no secret rooms of my heart anymore. I can't explain the joy I experienced in the midst of suffering. I know it was truly supernatural. I looked to God to work miracles and everyday He did.

My family is the love of my life and I am glad that I have been allowed to disclose this ugly secret of child sexual abuse so we can break the cycle of abuse for future generations. I've learned the power of intercessory prayer, going to God on other's behalf, because underneath the mask people wear are real people who are hurting and seeking love and acceptance. I learned that it is God's purpose to reconcile us to Himself through Christ so we can have a relationship of love and trust with Him.

## Pressing Forward

Statistics reported that 1 in 10 children are sexually abused before their 18th birthday. I was one of those children. My personal experiences with the trauma of childhood sexual abuse and the pain inflicted on the survivors, families and other loved ones prompted me to do something to prevent families from experiencing sexual abuse in the first place. My passion gave birth to me becoming a certified life coach and founding a non-profit organization, Maximizing God's Woman, Inc.

Maximizing God's Woman, Inc. is committed to preventing child sexual abuse by raising community awareness and igniting healthy relationships for women struggling with the long term effects of this type of abuse.

## Now That I Know

Although men have also suffered from child sexual abuse, we wanted to reach women who may be mothers of an abused child or partners of the perpetrators. From my experience I know these women struggle with the demands placed on them as the custodial parent trying to handle feelings of betrayal from someone they loved and trusted, and getting past the denial of what happened.

Our goal is to enable these women to talk about the abuse and to seek healing for themselves. It is only in exposing the dark secrets that we can stop the cycle of abuse. We believe all adults have a responsibility to speak up to dispel the shame and expose the darkness. I sincerely implore everyone to become informed and get involved. For more information, please visit us at www.maxgodswoman.org.

## *Whispers on My Journey*

***On my journey through the furnace
I heard a whisper –
"And we know that in all things God works
for the good of those who love Him, who have been called
according to His purpose."
Romans 8:28***

*I will never understand how God works but He never asked us to. He only requires us to believe, trust and obey Him. All my life I have been different, not that I wanted to be. Through my journey, I found my own voice and at last I began to love and appreciate me. What a beautiful thing!*

*Even while I was going through this journey, God was still blessing me in so many ways. I didn't know what He had planned for my life, but I knew it was something special. Not because of who I am but because God sent Jesus on a mission. Jesus said "the Spirit of the Lord is upon Me, because He has anointed Me to preach the gospel to the poor; He has sent Me to heal the brokenhearted, to proclaim liberty to the captives and recovery of sight to the blind; to set at liberty those who are oppressed, to proclaim the acceptable year of the Lord." Luke 4:18-19. I know that Jesus wants to set us all free from bondage.*

*Other people could have written this book or at least some of the chapters, but I was called to do it. For a long time, I didn't know my purpose. Now I'm on a mission to help protect the lives of innocent children from the fangs of perpetrators and help survivors to heal and break the cycle. I have been very transparent in this book in an effort to reveal how the enemy seeks to use child sexual abuse to "steal, kill and destroy" but God is greater and can turn the worst of situations around for our good and His glory. No, I don't understand it but I believe it because I've experienced it firsthand.*

*I know God is calling me to help others to be informed and get involved in protecting our precious little ones. As adults, we are responsible for their care. I only wish there were programs that helped perpetrators and not just imprison them. I will continue to cry aloud until others see the vision and take action.*

## Conclusion of the Matter

*Solomon, a very wise man stated:*

*Let us hear the conclusion of the whole matter:
Fear God, and keep His commandments:
for this is the whole duty of man.
For God shall bring every work into judgment,
with every secret thing,
whether it be good, or whether it be evil.*

*Ecclesiastes 12:13-14 (KJV)*

## End Notes

1. Child Maltreatment 2008 Report: Maltreatment Types of Victims. U. S. Department of Health and Human Services, Administration for Children & Families. (website: http//www.acf.hhs.gov/programs/cb/pubs/cm08/ table3_10.htm)

2. www.childwelfare.gov/pubs/use3rmanuals/foundation/founda-tionc.cfm